THE PERSONAGE
OF CHRIST

THE PERSONAGE OF CHRIST

*An In-depth Look at the God/Man Who is
Known of as Jesus of Nazareth . . .
That Human Being Individual Who is Also God Incarnate,
And Who Came to This Earth in Order to Pay An
Insurmountable Debt That He Personally Did Not Owe.*

Robert E. Daley

The Larry Czerwonka Company, LLC
Hilo, Hawai'i

For information email info@thelarryczerwonkacompany.com

First Edition — September 2015

This book is set in 14-point Garamond

Published by: The Larry Czerwonka Company, LLC
http://czerwonkapublishing.com

Printed in the United States of America

ISBN: 0692533699
ISBN-13: 978-0692533697

All scriptures used in this work are taken from the
King James Version of the Scriptures.

Contents

THE PERSONAGE

OF CHRIST

The Immutibility
of Counsel

Within a tract written by a man named Winkie Pratney, who is associated with the Last Day Ministries in Lindale, Texas, the mathematical precision of the Scripture is demonstrated through the work of a young Russian Harvard graduate named Ivan Panin, which was begun by Mr. Panin in 1882. Mr. Pratney's presentation is quite impressive and impacting. He goes on to say:

"The whole Bible is like this. I am just taking one small chunk of it and doing it in detail. Every paragraph, passage and book in the Bible can be shown to be constructed in the same marvelous way. What kind of fantastic collaboration between the disciples could have produced this structure without computers? How could mere fishermen and tax-collectors produce this kind of incredible structuring and design? What is crazy is that Mark is a Roman, Luke a Greek, and Matthew a Jew, but they all wrote with the same pattern. Each one wrote with their own unique flavor. Mark's style is different, but the pattern is the same right through! So who wrote it? One Mind, one Author . . . one God . . . many different writers, but one Writer. Can you imagine what kind of Mind would do this and not even care if you ever found out? What I want you to see is

how smart God is! These are not just words, it's an incredible mathematical pattern. It dances with its own poetry in mathematics. A computer would go into raptures over this! It's like a building where every piece joins perfectly into each other. And what is wild, is you can't pull even **one** *word out, without damaging the whole pattern. So the Bible carries within itself, a self-checking, self-verifying protection factor. If a person comes along and says I don't like this one, the whole pattern falls apart. This cannot be found in any other religious "holy" book in the world."*

* * *

On March 20, 1969, at a meeting of the Pediatric Society, a man named Dr. Richard L. Day . . . who had been an instruction professor since 1935 . . . and had just finished his term as National Medical Director of Planned Parenthood . . . and was currently a professor of pediatrics at the Mount Sinai School of Medicine . . . and who was considered an **insider** within something called **The Order** was quoted as saying:

"You will forget most or much of what I am going to tell you tonight . . . the old religions will have to go . . . especially Christianity. Then a new religion can be accepted for use all over the world. It will incorporate something from all of the old religions to make it more easy for people to accept and feel at home. Most

of the people will not be too concerned with religion. They will realize that they do not really need it.

In order to do this, the **Bible** *will be changed. It will be re-written to fit the new religion.*

Gradually, **key words** *will be replaced with new words having various shades of meaning.*

Then the meaning attached to the new word, can be close to the meaning of the old word . . . and as time goes on, other shades of meaning for that word, can be emphasized . . . and then gradually that word replaced with another word.

The few who do notice the difference will not be enough to matter . . . And, the churches will help us!"

It was stated that the idea within this calculated assault upon the Word of God, is that everything within the Scripture does not need to be rewritten . . . just certain **key words** to be replaced by other words.

The variability in meaning attached to any word can be used as a tool to change the **entire** meaning of the Scripture, and, therefore, make it acceptable to this *new* religion. Most of the people will not even know the difference.

It was also stated that Dr. Day was concerned that if what he had stated within that relaxed atmosphere ever really became known, that his days would be numbered. Within just a few months of informational release, Dr. Day was dead.

* * *

The whole of this study of The Deeper Things of God finds its basis within the unchanging Word of God, utilizing only the King James Version Translation of the Bible . . . and no other translation version will be acceptable for use within this study.

* * *

The supreme authority on the subject of God . . . is God Himself. He has granted unto us **"_all things_ that pertain unto life and godliness, through the knowledge of him that hath called us to glory and virtue."** *(II Peter 1:3b)*

Jesus of Nazareth said, **"Sanctify them through thy truth: thy word is truth."** *(John 17:17)*

Therefore, we will rely totally upon the written Word of God and upon the Word-of-God-supported Holy Spirit revelation, in the presenting of spiritual truth and existence realities. The Word of God itself testifies:

"The Law of the Lord is perfect, converting the soul: the testimony of the Lord is sure, making wise the simple.

The statutes of the Lord are right, rejoicing the heart: the commandment of the Lord is pure, enlightening the eyes.

The fear of the Lord is clean, enduring for ever: the judgments of the Lord are true and righteous altogether.

More to be desired are they than gold, yea, than much fine gold: sweeter also than honey and the honeycomb.

Moreover by them is thy servant warned: and in keeping of them there is great reward."
(Psalms 19:7-11)

* * *

"To the law and to the testimony: if they speak not according to this word, it is because there is no light in them." (Isaiah 8:20)

* * *

"So shall my word be that goeth forth out of my mouth: it shall not return unto me void, but it shall accomplish that which I please, and it shall prosper in the thing whereto I sent it." (Isaiah 55:11)

* * *

"For the word of God is quick, and powerful, and sharper than any two-edged sword, piercing even to the dividing asunder of soul and spirit, and of the joints and marrow, and is a discerner of the thoughts and intents of the heart." (Hebrews 4:12)

* * *

"Wherein God, willing more abundantly to show unto the heirs of promise the immutability of his counsel, confirmed it by an oath:

That by two immutable things, in which it was impossible for God to lie, we might have a strong consolation, who have fled for refuge to lay hold upon the hope set before us." (Hebrews 6:17-18)

* * *

"We have also a more sure word of prophecy; whereunto ye do well that ye take heed, as unto a light that shineth in a dark place, until the day dawn, and the day-star arise in your hearts:

Knowing this first, that no prophecy of the Scripture is of any private interpretation.

For the prophecy came not in old time by the will of man: but holy men of God spake as they were moved by the Holy Ghost." (II Peter 1:21)

* * *

The testimony of the Word of God applies to every subject or situation that we may encounter. The Word of God is our foundation . . . the Word of God is the bottom line . . . the Word of God is the end of the story . . . the Word of God is what God is. Everything that we will be looking at within our studies will find its foundation within the Word of God.

The Study of Christ

The *New Webster's Dictionary* defines:

Christ *noun*
> 1) lit. anointed
> 2) the Anointed One

The *Merriam Webster's Dictionary* defines:

Christ *noun*
> 1) MESSIAH
> 2) JESUS
> 3) an ideal type of Humanity
> 4) *Christian Science*: the ideal truth that comes as a divine manifestation of God to destroy incarnate error

* * *

God is the *infinite* Being that is the Creator of all things. Since the Word of God declares **"For with God nothing shall be impossible;"** *(Luke 1:37)* it follows that God is without restriction either by natural or supernatural limitations.

Man is a *finite* being . . . which means that he is restricted by natural and supernatural limitations. Man, *finite* and fallen from grace, cannot **_fully_** comprehend the *infinite* God because he has no understandable common point of reference to measure from, within the everlasting contexts that exist.

Christ is the *infinite* God, incarnated into a *finite* package of Humanity, with knowing limitations that ultimately extend to only that which is *non-transferable*.

* * *

As we begin our study of CHRIST we are able to reflect upon well-known verses of holy writ to substantiate that at a certain noted point in time, God sent to the planet Earth, the Personage of Christ, who is also declared to be His Son.

"For God so loved the world, that he gave his only begotten Son, that whosoever believeth in him should not perish, but have everlasting life." (John 3:16)

"But when the fulness of the time was finally come, God sent forth his Only Begotten Son, made of a Human woman, made under the Law of Moses requirements," (Galatians 4:4; Enhanced)

When we are talking about *The Christ*, we are talking about a particular, singular individual, which by his very title is the only divinely *Anointed One*, out of the projected myriad of Human candidates that are constantly being referred to and put forth by other Human Beings.

"In him was spiritual *life; and the* spiritual *life was the light of men.*

And the light shineth in spiritual *darkness; and the* spiritual *darkness comprehended it not."*
(John 1:4-5; Enhanced)

The Christ is unique. The Christ is anointed of God. The Christ is appointed to perform a very specific task. The Christ is the legal representative of the whole of Humanity. The Christ is the nemesis of the *"god of this world"* (II Corinthians 4:4) and the divine representative of the conflict that exists between the kingdom of Light and the kingdom of Darkness. The Christ is the embodiment of *Life, Light,* and *Love* within a *Human-Suit* of flesh. The Christ is a prophetical prototype of a New Species of Human Being.

Before the Incarnation

B efore the beginning of anything . . . God is. **NOTHING** precedes God: Nothing comes before God. Nothing exists before God.

There is no *Beginning* before God.

There is no *Time* before God.

There is no *Creation* before God.

Existence is . . . but The Personage of God is the totality of all *Existence*.

The Personage of God is . . . but there is NOTHING else.

* * *

"Through faith we understand that the worlds that exist *were framed by the word of God, so that* the *things which are seen were not made of* the *things which do appear."* (Hebrews 11:3; Enhanced)

"For the <u>invisible things</u> of him from the creation of the world are clearly seen, being understood by the things that are made, even concerning *his eternal power and <u>Godhead</u>; so that they* all *are without excuse:"* (Romans 1:20; Enhanced)

So what *"invisible things"* might we be able to understand concerning decisions and actions that were most assuredly taken by the Members of the *"God-head"* at this point?

And, keep in mind that when we are looking at **The Christ** we are looking at one of the Members of the Godhead clothed in a *Human-Suit* of flesh. Notations of actions that were taken *Before the Beginning,* where **The Christ** is involved, are underlined.

1) Since within the One God Godhead there are Three Members . . . a decision needs to be amicably arrived at, concerning who will occupy the equality Position number One . . . and <u>**who will occupy the equality Position number Two**</u> . . . and who will occupy the equality Position number Three.

2) Since by Divine design there shall be three different full and active operational Realms of Existence brought forth . . . emanating directly from the very God which is the fullness of existence . . . a decision needs to be amicably arrived at, concerning the operational order of those Three Realms . . . and <u>**who will be the Head of, and Administrator of,**</u>

each particular Realm of *Thought*, **_Word_**, and *Deed*.

3) Since by Divine design, and because of granted free-will moral agency, there shall be three valid States of Being for moral creation to reside in . . . those designated conditions need to become established, manifest, and secured even before one free-will moral creature is brought forth. Those **States of Being** include . . . the State of Being **Immortal**, which is the reality of being untouchable by any of the aspects of death when it comes forth . . . and the State of Being **Eternal**, which is the reality of having the capacity to live forever if continued obedience is chosen . . . and the State of Being **Mortal**, which is the reality of being death-doomed without reprieve.

4) Since within the One God Godhead there shall be various responsibilities and task-assignments that shall need to be performed by each of the Three Members . . . several decisions need to be amicably arrived at concerning **_who will handle and then be held accountable for various specific tasks._**

**And it must further be agreed upon that no One Member will cross-over any of the designated lines of separated-task-assignment responsibilities.**

5) Since the Three Members of the One God Godhead are not at all confused or befuddled concerning who they are . . . but Mankind, when it is brought forth, is certain to be unclear concerning who is actually who . . . _**titles and names need to be amicably arrived at for each of the Three Members**_ according to their assigned responsibilities.

6) Since the aspect of free-will decision for all of moral creation shall become the centermost issue within all of Existence . . . and since Divine Foreknowledge _(Isaiah 46:10)_ is already aware of the two major rebellions that shall come forth within the two Probationary Periods that will occur . . . there needs to be the drafting of two specific Plans of Redemption and Reconciliation that shall be made available for acceptance to _whosoever_ requires them. _**The Plan of Redemption is designed for Mankind, which requires the application and usage of the physical**_

element of Blood for ratification . . . and a Plan of Reconciliation is designed for all *Angelic Hosts* and all *Other Creatures*, which does not require the usage of the Blood element.

7) When we understand that there are restoration opportunities that shall be provided for broken relationships, we should also understand that a set of accurate records need to be prepared and preserved for *fairness* purposes. *There shall be a single Book of Life prepared for the accurate name preservation of every single Express Image creature of the Living God that exists among the constituency of Mankind* *(Hebrews 1:3)* *who has chosen the path of life-everlasting through Jesus Christ of Nazareth.* And there shall be prepared, a set of other *Books* that contain accurate record-keeping of all errant activities of Human moral creation run amok. *(Revelation 20:12)*

8) *A superior project of divine design that within the process of Time will actually deal with an unprecedented creation of a new-species of moral being, shall be*

prophetically drafted in liquid silver and dipped in transparent gold by the creative hand of predestination. (Romans 8:29) **All of the details concerning this project are fully completed and in order even before one-second of created Time ticks by. Everything having to do with this particular project is finished ahead of Time because the whole of this project is accomplished by the full Personage of God through the future God/Man, and for the benefit of the New Creation new-species constituents that shall be birthed into it. Simple belief and acceptance of what God has done is the initial requirement of entrance.** (John 6:29) **Willful continued obedience and adherence to regulation mandates will fully seal the off the charts benefits that go with this plan.** (Revelation 17:14)

9) Since God is a Creator and not a magician, of necessity the creation-regulation restrictions . . . or the creative laws by which all things shall be brought forth into existence, and then operate by, need to be drafted, established, and installed. This includes the

initial base-set of laws (both spiritual and natural) and also whatsoever associate supportive laws that might apply that will work harmoniously and cooperatively with those base-set of laws.

$$* \quad * \quad *$$

Within our study of **The Christ**, it must be first understood that we are talking about, and dealing with, the reality of the Second Person of the Godhead actually becoming a Human Being . . . for the purpose of salvaging the immense amount of investment that the Godhead has made in creating a creature *"in"* their own image, and *"after"* their own likeness.

We are foundationally dealing with Divinity. That is: we are dealing with **Light**, *(I John 1:5)* **Love**, *(I John 4:8) and* **Life**, *(John 1:4, Mark 10:45, John 5:26; 6:48; 10:10; 11:25; 14:6, and I John 1:2, 5:20)* choosing to step away from the *non-transferable* qualities of Omnipotence . . . and Omniscience . . . and Omnipresence <u>forever</u> . . . in order to step into a prepared *Human-Suit* of flesh, and redeem all of Humanity . . . simply because of pure, unselfish Love.

The pre-incarnate Christ is indeed, fully the Second Person of the unfathomable operating Godhead.

Prior to the incarnation *(i.e., Divinity putting on Humanity)* the Second Person of the Godhead was

Omni-potently, powerfully, able to do all things . . . and Omnisciently, intuitively, able to know all things . . . and Omni-presently, active, and able to make His very presence known and felt everywhere at the same time.

After the incarnation, **The Christ** is still the Second Person of, and an in-good-standing Member of, the Divine Godhead:

But as a Human Being, he is able to powerfully accomplish <u>only</u> that which is facilitated through the Divine *power-portion* operation of the Third Person of the Godhead whom we know of as the Holy Spirit of God . . . *just like any other Man within Humanity.*

And as a Human Being, he is able to be knowledgeable of *(other than what can be learned through standard growth and study)* only that which is revealed to him by the Third Person of the Godhead whom we know of as the Holy Spirit of God, utilizing the Holy Spirit giftings that are spoken of within I Corinthians, chapter 12 . . . *just like any other Man within Humanity.*

And instead of being a Divine *facilitator* of the quality of Omnipresence . . . he is now, as a Human Being, become *inclusive within* the actual operation of the Divine quality of Omnipresence, *just like any other Man within the New Creation portion of Humanity, which has become Born-Again and is indwelt by the Holy Spirit of God.*

A Walk Along the Path of Humanity

" *I* will **raise them up** an *anointed* **Prophet from among their brethren, like unto thee** *Moses,* **and will put my words in his mouth; and he shall speak unto them all that I shall command** *of him to speak.*

And it shall come to pass, that whosoever *from among all of Mankind that* **will not hearken unto my words which he shall speak in my name, I will** *surely* **require it of him.**" *(Deuteronomy 18:18-19; Enhanced)*

"**But when the fulness of the time was** *finally* **come, God sent forth his** *Only Begotten* **Son, made of a** *Human* **woman, made under the Law** *of Moses re*quirements," *(Galatians 4:4; Enhanced)*

"**Wherefore in all things it behooved him to be made like unto his brethren** *in every respect,* **that he might be**come **a merciful and faithful High Priest in things pertaining to God, to** *be able to* **make reconciliation for the sins of the people.**" *(Hebrews 2:17; Enhanced)*

The Second Person of the Godhead has now stepped away from heaven and most of the *non-transferables* . . . and put on a *Human-Suit* of flesh . . . and become a Man. His walk with Humanity literally begins with a normal gestation process of his prepared body *(Hebrews 10:5)* and an unnoticeable orchestrated birth.

As an infant, his necessary nurturers and protectors are Mary his birth mother and Joseph his mother's husband. After their demonstrated-obedience in fulfilling the Law of Moses, *which included his circumcision on the 8th day of his life, his presentation unto the Lord as the child that openeth the womb, and his mother's sacrifice for her issue of blood purification, (Luke 2:18; 22-24; 39)* the family returned unto Nazareth to begin their life together. *(Luke 2:39)*

An unexpected royal visit by Middle-Eastern Magi two years later concludes with the Lord directing Joseph, through a dream, to take his family into Egypt for protection until he is instructed otherwise. *(Matthew 2:13-15)* When King Herod the Great, and all of those who were in league with him to destroy the Messiah, were finally dead . . . Joseph is instructed, once again through a dream, to return unto the town of Nazareth so that a normal family life-routine is able to occur. *(Matthew 2:19-23)*

Special Notation: *The Second Person of the Godhead's dealings with Humanity did not commence in the Old Testament* *with His interacting with a Burning Bush . . . or with Him becoming Melchizdek the priest of God . . . nor with Him being the Fourth Man within a burning fiery furnace during the days of Daniel, as is so often put forth.*

* * *

"And <u>being found in fashion as a man,</u> he *willingly* **humbled himself, and became obedient unto death, even the** *spiritual and physical* **death of the cross."** *(Philippians 2:8; Enhanced)*

At the age of twelve years . . . an astounding revelation is given unto a young Jesus of Nazareth, setting him on a new course of action for the rest of his life. Although it is usually quite difficult for most people to accept . . . up until the time that he is twelve years of age, Jesus of Nazareth does not really know who he is. He is unaware of the reality that he is God, manifest in the flesh. Within his mind he is simply an obedient, normal, pre-teen, young Jewish man.

At a Feast of Passover celebration, while his parents were involved with the adult feast activities, the Holy Spirit of God utilizing the gifting of the Word of Knowledge *(1 Corinthians 12:8)* reveals to a twelve year old Jesus that he is actually the Second Person of the Godhead living within a *Human-Suit* of flesh. *(Philippians 2:8)*

That revelation is so much more than difficult to fully grasp, and to attempt to understand just what that must have been like for Jesus.

When the Feast of Passover is concluded, and the worshipping faithful are on their way back home unto the city of Nazareth . . . Jesus is missing. This action of independency is unprecedented and has never happened before. His parents are understandably concerned. And leaving the traveling troupe of pilgrims, Joseph and Mary return unto the city of Jerusalem to find him. Three days and three nights of searching finally yield results, as they once again check the temple area.

"And when they saw him, they were totally amazed: and his mother said unto him, Son, why hast thou thus dealt with us? Behold, thy father and I have sought thee sorrowing.

And he said unto them, How is it that ye sought me? Wist ye not that I must be about my Heavenly Father's business?" (Luke 2:48-49; Enhanced)

The response to his mother's statement concerning Jesus' incredulous behavior indicates that he is genuinely surprised that his parents do not actually know who he is. He is only twelve . . . and they are fully adult. He has just found out who he really is . . . and they do not even know? Parents are supposed to be more knowledgeable than their children, and yet, when it comes to this particular issue . . . they do not really know? No . . . ! No one did.

And the Apostle Paul in his epistle to the believers in the city of Corinth confirms unto us that Mary, Joseph, the shepherds, the Magi, John the Baptist, the disciples, and whosoever else there may have been, <u>never</u> did know who Jesus of Nazareth really was during the entire time of his ministerial activities here on this Earth.

"Which none of the princes *of the darkness* **of this world knew: for had they** *truly* **known** *of it,* **they would not** *ever* **have crucified the Lord of glory."**
(I Corinthians 2:8; Enhanced)

The realities that are being dealt with here are very, very serious issues. They are much more serious than most people ever realize. The kingdom of darkness is the kingdom, at the time of **The Christ**, which is currently in control over this entire world. Adam bowed his knee unto Satan through obedience to the serpent's suggestion, and put himself in subjection to the dark lord of evil. *(Romans 6:16)* That captivity to Sin has been passed on down the road even unto us today. The authority that was given unto Adam from God is now able to be accessed by Satan and his company toadies using unsuspecting Human individuals. To reverse this grim situation, God must act legally, openly, and promptly.

Even though young Jesus is only twelve years of age . . . eternal, universal, spiritual realities are on the line. Just as the Scripture states . . . had the unholy, fallen-angelic princes of this current Social Order, world-system, <u>known</u> who Jesus of Nazareth really was, they would not have come anywhere near him.

The Human-generated, emotional override of "after all Pastor Rob, Mary was his mother and she was spoken to by an angel at his incarnation, surely she should know" . . . or . . . "after all Pastor Rob, John the Baptist was God's sanctioned prophet on the scene, he certainly should know" . . . or . . . "after all Pastor Rob, Peter was his ministerial right-hand man and was closer to him than anyone else, and God even revealed to him that he was *The Christ*, he must have known" do not even come into the picture.

At the time of *The Christ*, the Devil currently has the keys of Death and of Hell, *(Revelation 1:18)* and God is not going to leave it that way. Jesus is the only hope that there is for this lost and dying world.

* * *

At thirty years of age, Jesus emerges out of Scriptural silence and manifests upon the scene. He has spent the last eighteen years developing sensitivity to the gentle unctioning of the Holy Spirit; and increasing exponentially in his knowledge of the Word of God. Mental attempts to determine what other endeavors he may have accomplished are summarily without value.

On a given day in the fall of a given year, the Holy Spirit delivers unto Jesus a Word of Wisdom, *(1 Corinthians 12:8)* that it is time to go down to the River Jordan in the south, and encounter the Baptist. *(Matthew 3:13)*

* * *

"Now when all *of* the people were baptized," *(Luke 3:21a; Enhanced)* . . . indicates to us that on the particular day that Jesus of Nazareth arrives at the Jordan River, John the Baptist had been in the process of ministering repentance and cleansing, through water baptism, to whosoever would come unto him . . . as he was normally wont to do. And by the time that Jesus shows up on the scene, whosoever came to be baptized on that day had accomplished their task, and had moved on to the other activities that might be scheduled on their agenda. No one was actually there at the river except John, who was possibly sitting and warming himself by the fire.

As Jesus approaches, John stands up and begins to move toward the river, knowing for what purpose the stranger that was coming to him was there for. By the time that Jesus reaches the river and removes his sandals, John has already backed into the water up to his thighs. Scripturally speaking, ***"He hath no*** *special* ***form nor comeliness; and when we shall see him, there is no beauty*** *nor attractiveness* ***that we should desire him."*** *(Isaiah 53:2b; Enhanced)* So, John does <u>not</u> know that Jesus is any different than anyone else who has ever come to him for baptism. There is no glowing halo around his head as is in the pictures, and there is no personal recognition from John simply because they are proposed to be *cousins* . . . they are from different Hebrew tribes. Jesus slowly approaches John until both of them are a little deeper than their waist in the water. John speaks to Jesus, as he has to thousands of others, concerning the purpose of water baptism . . . at which point Jesus is then immersed into the water and baptized.

> ***"And*** *afterward* ***Jesus, when he was baptized, went up straightway out of the water: and, lo, the heavens were opened unto him, and he*** *(i.e. John the Baptist)* ***saw the Spirit of God descending like a dove, and lighting upon him:***
>
> ***And lo a voice from*** *the Father, coming from* ***heaven, saying, This is my beloved Son, in whom I am well pleased."*** *(Matthew 3:16-17; Enhanced)*

John himself testifies *"And I personally **knew him not: but he that sent me to baptize** people **with water, the same said unto me, Upon whom thou shalt see the** Holy **Spirit descending, and remaining on him, the same is he which baptizeth** people **with the Holy Ghost."** *(John 1:33; Enhanced)*

With the descent of the Holy Spirit in the form of a dove, John suddenly realizes in whose presence he is actually standing. He has been baptizing hundreds of people for months now, and finally, the one that he was told to look for by God is standing right next to him. So . . . in a contrite and humble manner . . . *"John forbad him, saying, I have need to be baptized of thee, and comest thou to me?*

And Jesus answering said unto him, Suffer it to be so for **now: for thus it becometh us to fulfil all righteousness. Then he suffered him."** *(Matthew 3:14-15; Enhanced)*

John goes on to testify *"And I personally **knew him not: but that he should be made manifest to Israel** as the God-ordained Messiah**, therefore am I come baptizing with water.**

And John bare record of Jesus**, saying I saw the** Holy **Spirit descending from heaven like a dove, and it abode upon him.**

*And I truly **saw, and bare record that this is the Son of God."** (John 1:31-32, 34; Enhanced)*

"And immediately the *Holy* **Spirit driveth him into the wilderness."** *(Mark 1:12; Enhanced)*

The entire purpose for the Water Baptism of Jesus of Nazareth was to clearly reveal God's chosen deliverer to his ordained Prophet-on-the-scene named John. *(Amos 3:7)* Jesus himself was not in any real need of repentance. And in the not-too-distant future, a veritable change in Prophetal Position shall take place as John decreases and Jesus increases.

* * *

"And Jesus being fully *cloaked* **of the Holy Ghost returned from Jordan, and was led by the** *Holy* **Spirit into the wilderness,**
There **being forty days tempted of the devil. And in those days he did eat** *and drink* **nothing. And when they were ended, he afterward hungered.**
And the devil *whispered into his ear and* **said unto him, IF thou be the Son of God, command this stone that it be made bread."** *(Luke 4:1-3; Enhanced)*

It is time for Jesus to prove himself . . . is it not? After all, he receives a revelation when he is twelve years of age concerning who he really is. He has studied

the Scriptures for the past eighteen years, and they testify clearly of him being the Chosen One. Now he has
visited the Prophet of God and received a confirmation of his calling . . . his Humanity-ego is being
tempted to substantiate the validity of all of these
truths. Just prove it! No one is ever going to know.
No one is watching. This is the wilderness . . . no one
is even here!

Special Notation: *May the Lord help us to make the
jump to light-speed at this juncture? We are dealing with a
100% Human Man here. Yes, a Man who is without flaws.
Yes, a perfect Man. Yes, an ideal Man. Just the kind of a Man
that God originally desired and created in the first place . . . but
still yet . . . a Human Man. Hello?*

*When it comes to Jesus, and particularly in our observ-
ing him concerning how we are supposed to operate and behave,
we need to get the God-ness out of our mind! We need to focus
on his Humanity. "But Pastor Rob, he is God!" Well of course
he is . . . and there is nothing that he can do to <u>not</u> be God. He
has always been God. He is God right now. He always will be
God. He cannot help it! That is who he really is. But he is not
here on this Earth functioning as God. He is not operating right
now as God. He is not ministering among men as God. He is
not living his day to day life . . . just like you and I currently
live our day to day life . . . as God. He is living his life as a
Man. He is thinking as a Man. He is hoping as a Man. He is*

using the restroom as a Man. He is saddened as a Man. He is challenged as a Man. He is tempted as a Man. He is demonstrating that the creature called MAN really can do it! Man can be successful. Man can be victorious. Man can be responsible. Man can walk sin free. Man can be accountable. Man can substantiate that he is capable of ruling and managing the affairs of this whole universe just as he was originally designed. And at least one of the reasons that Jesus is here . . . is to prove just that.

Jesus does not yield to the soulish-ego of self, but rather chooses to:

"Submit yourselves therefore *unto* **God.** *Choose to* **resist the devil, and he will flee from you."** *(James 4:7; Enhanced)*

"And Jesus answered him, saying, It is written *that***, Man shall not live by bread alone, but by every word that proceedeth** *forth* **out of the mouth of God."** *(Matthew 4:4; Enhanced)*

Ding, ding, ding . . . Round #1 goes to Jesus.

"And the devil, taking him up into a high mountain *in the spirit***, showed unto him all the kingdoms of the world in a** *brief* **moment of time.**

And the devil said unto him, All *of* **this power will I give** *unto* **thee, and the glory of them** *all***: for**

that power **is <u>delivered unto me</u>** *by Adam;* **and to whomsoever I will** *choose to,* **I give it.**

If thou therefore wilt worship me, all *of this* **shall be thine."** *(Luke 4:5-7; Enhanced)*

Well, how about that? <u>All</u> of the earthly kingdoms that this Probationary Period would produce. Power . . . Authority . . . Riches . . . Lusts of the flesh . . . Influence . . . Jesus, you could be the Top-Dog over all of the Earth.

Where did Satan get this kind of authority from in the first place? Where did Satan get this kind of control over the kingdoms of this Earth? *<u>From Adam!!</u>*

"Know ye not, that to whom <u>ye yield your-selves</u> servants to obey, his servants ye are to whom ye obey; whether of sin unto death, or of obedience unto righteousness." *(Romans 6:16)*

Jesus of Nazareth has come as a man, to get back what the devil originally got from Adam. Should Jesus fall prey to the seduction of power, riches, and self-exaltation, then Satan will remain ensconced in a position of usurped-power and authority over men forever.

"And Jesus answered and said unto him, Get thee behind me, Satan: for it is written, Thou

shalt worship the Lord thy God, and him only shalt thou serve." *(Luke 4:8)*

Ding, ding, ding . . . Round #2 goes to Jesus.

*"And he brought him to Jerusalem in the spirit, and set him on a pinnacle of the temple, and said unto him, **IF** thou be the Son of God, cast thyself down from hence.*

For it is written, He shall give his angels charge over thee, to keep thee.

And in their hands they shall bear thee up, lest at any time thou dash thy foot against a stone." *(Luke 4:9-11; Enhanced—Satan's quote is a paraphrase of Psalms 91:11-12)*

Once again the Humanity-ego of the Man named Jesus of Nazareth is being challenged . . . as concerning who he really is . . . the *Last Adam*. *(I Corinthians 15:45)* Satan is endeavoring to use the Scriptural Word of Truth that Jesus has successfully rebutted him with on two previous occasions. To attempt suicide, with a Scriptural promise of divine intervention, is what is suggested.

"And Jesus answering said unto him, It is said, Thou shalt not tempt the Lord thy God." *(Luke 4:12)*

Ding, ding, ding . . . Round #3, and the final decision for this encounter, goes to Jesus.

God has designed Man to rule. But He did not design Man to begin his ruler-ship apart from being closely connected to Him. An invisible, spiritual-umbilical-cord connected the heart of God directly to the heart of Adam. And in all that Adam was to authoritatively do, he was to first check with his God. And please understand that this initiating connection-scenario would not be a forever and ever situation. However, until the Father and the son reached a point where they *thought* as if they were only one, and *talked* as if they were only one, and even *acted* as if they were only one, this umbilical would stay in place. When Adam sinned, he chose to sever the umbilical cord and run away from home.

In Jesus, we have a 100% Human Man who is being put through the ringer by the opposing forces, to see if he will capitulate like his earlier predecessor. Concerning the Temptation in the Wilderness, Jesus passes the test. But that desert sojourn is not where it ended . . .

"And when the devil had ended all *of* the temptations, he departed from him <u>for a little season</u>."
(Luke 4:13; Enhanced)

* * *

One of the most bodacious portions of Scripture . . . within the Sin-defiled mind of Man . . . can be found within the eighty-second Psalm. Never, in forty-years of being a Christian, has this author ever heard of anyone who has summed up enough courage to touch upon these passages. But Jesus, our Lord, did. *(John 10:34-38)* And Jesus was speaking truthfully from a position of insight and wisdom concerning not just the here and now but the innumerable eons that are to come as well.

"God standeth in the congregation of the mighty, he judgeth among the gods *that He hath made.*

How long will ye judge unjustly, and accept the persons of the wicked? *How long?* **Selah.**

Purpose to **defend the poor and** *the* **fatherless.** *Determine to* **do justice to the afflicted and** *the* **needy.**

Commit thyself to **deliver the poor and** *the* **needy,** *and* **rid them out of the hand of the wicked.**

They know not *concerning spiritual truth,* **neither will they understand. They** *continue to* **walk on in darkness. All** *of* **the foundations of the earth are out of course.**

I have said *with My mouth,* <u>**Ye are gods;**</u> **and all of you** *that are redeemed* **are** *indeed* <u>**children of the Most High.**</u>

But ye shall die *just* **like** *mere* **men, and** *even* **fall like one of the princes.**

Arise, O God *of grace,* **and judge the earth. For thou shalt inherit all** *of the* **nations** *during your Millennial Reign.* **"** *(Psalm 82:1-8; Enhanced)*

"Jesus answered them, Is it not written in your law, I said, Ye are gods?

If he called <u>them</u> **gods, unto whom the word of God came,** *i.e. the Nation of Israel,* **and the Scripture cannot be broken;**

Say ye of him, whom the Father hath sanctified, and sent into the world, Thou blasphemest; because I said, I am the Son of God?

If I do not the works of my Father, believe me not.

But if I do, though ye believe not me, believe the works; that ye may know, and believe, that the Father is in me, and I in him." *(John 10:34-38; Enhanced)*

Special Notation: *Shall we believe the Scriptures, or not? Shall we believe a man who never tells us a lie, or not? Shall we believe what our own eyes are able to clearly read here, or not? Which will it be? When will we reach that place that we will choose to believe? What is it going to take to make us let go of the past (which can never be changed) and embrace the reality of the now and the promise of the future ahead? How long are* *we going to carry around the sack that is slung over our shoulder, that is full of past shortcomings, mistakes, lies, falsehoods, misconceptions, innuendos, vileness, heinousness, and death? How long??*

As Jesus **_WAS_** {when he walked **_"after the flesh"_** *(II Corinthians 5:16a)*}, **_YOU_** can become . . . today . . . right now! As Jesus **_IS_** {whom **_"know we him no more"_** *(II Corinthians 5:16b)*} as a New, Manifested, Spiritual, Glorified, Species of Human Creation, **_YOU_** shall become . . . in the not-too-distant future! So, what are we waiting for?

* * *

When Jesus emerges from the wilderness, John is still baptizing people in water, and has just been challenged by the priests and the Levites that were sent from Jerusalem. John bears witness to them concerning the Messiah, and what he has personally seen and heard only a short while ago.

"The next day John seeth Jesus *as he is* **_coming unto him, and saith_** *prophetically,* **_Behold the Lamb of God, which taketh away the sin of the world!"_** *(John 1:29; Enhanced)*

This is **not** a statement of personal insight. Remember, John does not really know who Jesus is. At this point in time he believes that Jesus is the Messiah . . . the One who will bring deliverance from the Roman yoke of bondage . . . but he does not know that Jesus is God manifest in a *Human-Suit* of flesh. His statement is a Prophetical Declaration, uttered by the operating ordained Prophet of God on the scene.

> **"Again the next day after** *the first***, John stood, and two of his** *faithful* **disciples;**
>
> **And** *once again* **looking upon Jesus as he walked, he saith, Behold the Lamb of God!**
>
> **And the two disciples heard him speak, and** *immediately they left off following John and* **they followed** *after* **Jesus."** *(John 1:35-37; Enhanced)*

Andrew and John the Beloved, the younger son of Zebedee, were disciples of John the Baptist. As fishermen, they were *blue-collar* workers to be sure . . . but they were also spiritually inclined and interested in the things of eternal value.

When they hear their spiritual-mentor John the Baptist declare that the One whom he has been bearing witness of as being the Messiah was there . . . they immediately left off following John and took up following Jesus. Andrew is excited about the turn-of-events, and immediately locates his brother Simon, who is not very far away . . . but who is not really interested in spiritual issues. Andrew persuades Simon to at least come and check Jesus out . . . and Jesus' Word of Knowledge *(I Corinthians 12:8)* concerning Simon catches his attention.

The next day Jesus is scheduled to return to the Galilee region, to fulfill a previous commitment of a wedding feast invitation for family friends.

As Jesus is about to leave the Judea region, he **"findeth Philip, and saith unto him, Follow me.**

Now Philip was of Bethsaida *in the north***, the city of Andrew and Peter.**

Philip *immediately went out and* **findeth Nathanael, and saith unto him, We have found him, of whom Moses in the law, and the prophets, did write, Jesus of Nazareth, the son of Joseph.**

And Nathanael said unto him, Can there any good thing *really* **come out of Nazareth? Philip saith unto him, Come and see.**

Jesus saw Nathanael coming to him, and *under the Holy Spirit gifting of the Word of Knowledge* **saith of him, Behold an Israelite indeed in whom is no guile!**

Nathanael saith unto him, Whence knowest thou me? Jesus answered and said unto him, Before

that Philip called thee, when thou wast under the fig tree, I saw thee.

Nathanael answered and saith unto him, Rabbi, thou art the Son of God, thou art the King of Israel.

Jesus answered and said unto him, Because I said unto thee, I saw thee under the fig tree, believest thou? Thou shalt see greater things than these.

And he saith unto him, Verily, verily, I say unto you, Hereafter ye shall see heaven open, and the angels of God ascending and descending upon the Son of man." (John 1:43-51; Enhanced)

Jesus has acquired his *First-Five* disciples, only one of which he personally called. At this point in time, it would seem that they all desire to be with him . . . so together they leave the Judea region and travel toward the north, entering into the Galilee region where Jesus was raised-up from the time that he was a small child.

The marriage feast that Jesus and his family were invited to was already in progress by the time that Jesus and his disciples arrive in Galilee. Jesus is not a rude individual, and would not attempt to impose himself upon friends or family with the men that have come with him. It would again seem probable that in some manner, Jesus is seen in the area, and the governor of the wedding feast is approached and informed that Jesus is here, but that he has five uninvited men along with him. The governor of the feast graciously extends an invitation, *"and both Jesus was called, and his disciples, to the marriage."* (John 2:2)

The marriage feast is delightful. Fellowship, camaraderie, and congratulations abound as guests and participants both enjoy the covenant commitment festivities. At a given point in time the wine is all consumed, and Mary comes to Jesus as a Jewish mother would, and subtly suggests that he assist as a matter of courtesy. Jesus has not yet officially stepped into public ministry, and he attempts to sidestep the suggestion. Typically, a Jewish mother will not be put off . . . so Mary simply turns to the servants and instructs them to do whatever Jesus would command. All eyes now shift to Jesus, and the pressure of expectancy awaits his directive.

"Fill the waterpots to the top with water." (John 2:7a; Enhanced)

"Draw out now, and bear unto the governor of the feast." (John 2:8b)

"When the ruler of the feast had tasted the water that was made wine, and knew not from whence it was; but the servants which drew the

water knew, the governor of the feast called the bridegroom.

And saith unto him, Every man at the beginning of the feast doth set forth good wine; and when men have well drunk, then that wine which is worse: but thou hast kept the good wine until now. (John 2:9-10; Enhanced)

Here we have the first recorded miracle that is attributed to Jesus of Nazareth. It is not often recognized that what we have is actually the Holy Spirit Gift of the *Working of Miracles (I Corinthians 12:9)* in operation here. Jesus is a Man. Men do not perform miracles. God performs miracles. Jesus is indeed God. But Jesus is not operating as God while he is here on this Earth. God, the Holy Spirit, is actually the one who is working through the Man Jesus of Nazareth to perform this miracle. *(I Corinthians 12:10)* But Jesus is the one who is getting the credit, both then and now.

* * *

Special Notation: Men are <u>not</u> usually impressed when God works a miracle because after all . . . He is God . . . He can do anything. However, men <u>are</u> usually impressed when they believe that other men are working miracles, because they attribute these men to be God-Like and superior to them. They will *then listen to what these men have to say, and will be affected accordingly. And even though the sin-defiled character of these men may manifest as being questionable . . . the resulting glory for the miracle will erroneously be given unto them.*

During the upcoming Tribulation Period the false prophet (through the assistance of Satan,) will supposedly work miracles, which will arrest the attention of other men and persuade them that the Antichrist and the False Prophet are God-Like and superior to them. The affecting end-result will not be good.

New Creation saints of God should be operating with the Working of Miracles today, as the Holy Spirit gifts them. Their character should reflect a cleansing of spiritual filth, a putting off of the Old and a putting on of the New, and a laying aside of weight and easily besetting sin. Other men will then attribute these saints as being God-Like and superior to them. They will then listen to what these men have to say, and will be affected accordingly unto righteousness and true holiness.

* * *

When the marriage feast is over, Jesus takes his family on a scouting trip to the city of Capernaum to look for new ministerial headquarters. *(Matthew 4:13)* Peter and Andrew and John return to their fishing business as employees of Zebedee. Philip and Nathanael move on unto other endeavors, and Jesus is once again without any disciples.

"And the Jews' Feast *of* **Passover** *was at hand, and Jesus went up to Jerusalem* alone,

And he **found in the temple those that sold oxen and sheep and doves, and** the **changers of money sitting.**

And when he had made a scourge of small cords, he drove them all out of the temple, and the sheep, and the oxen; and poured out the changers' money, and overthrew the tables;

And said unto them that sold doves, Take these things hence; make not my Father's house a house of merchandise.

(Verse 17 is non-applicable)

Then answered the Jews and said unto him, What sign of authority **showest thou unto us, seeing that thou doest these things?**

Jesus answered and said unto them, Destroy this temple, and in three days I will raise it up.

Then said the Jews, Forty and six years was this temple of Solomon **in the building** thereof, **and will thou rear it up** again **in three days?**

But he spakc unto them **of the temple of his body."** (John 2:13-21; Enhanced)

(Verse 22 is non-applicable)

* * *

From the *Cleansing of the Temple* for the first time, *(John 2:14-21)* through the *Unrecorded Miracles* that he did in Jerusalem, *(John 2:23)* and the *Visitation of Nicodemus*, *(John 3:1-21)* on to his *Return into Galilee for a Ministration of Power and Teaching*, *(Luke 4:14-15)* and his entering into an unnamed city in Galilee and the *Healing of a Leper*, *(Luke 5:12-15)* . . . to his *Official Entrance into Public Ministry* within the synagogue in the city of Nazareth, *(Luke 4:16-30)* and his *Deliverance of a Demon-Possessed Man* in the synagogue within the city of Capernaum, *(Luke 4:31-36)* unto his utilization of Captain Simon's boat to land an enormous *Draught of Fishes*, *(Luke 5:1-10)* and finally to his *Calling of Four Men* to follow him—Jesus is ministering, **without any disciples**.

No one is there to testify about him at the *Cleansing of the Temple* in Jerusalem. No one is there to *back-him-up* at his *Official Entrance into Public Ministry* in Nazareth. No one was there when he *Healed the Leper* in an unnamed city. No one was there to confirm within the *Galilee Ministration* concerning anything that he has done. Other than the *First-Five* that he had acquired after the wilderness temptations, and who left him after the wedding feast . . . there are **<u>no disciples</u>** with Jesus up until he calls the *Faithful-Four*.

*"**And as Jesus** was **walking by the sea of Galilee**, he saw two brethren, **Simon called Peter, and Andrew***

his brother, casting a net into the sea: for they were fishers.

And he saith unto them, Follow me, and I will make you *to be* fishers of men.

And they straightway left their nets *inside their boat*, and followed him.

And going on *down the shoreline* from thence, he saw an*other* two brethren, *who were* James the son of Zebedee, and John his *younger* brother, in a ship with Zebedee their father, mending their nets *of the brake that occurred when they landed the draught of fishes;* and he called them.

And they *both* immediately left the ship and their father, and followed him." *(Matthew 4:18-22; Enhanced)*

This is not the first time that Peter and Andrew and John have come into contact with Jesus. They were a part of the *First-Five*; and had seen him change water into wine at a wedding feast in Cana and had recently landed a large Draught of Fishes when he borrowed Simon's boat. This time . . . they have left their nets for good.

"And as he passed by *the taxation scales*, he saw Levi the son of Alpheus, *who is also known of as Matthew*, sitting at the receipt of custom, and said unto *him, Follow me. And he* immediately **arose and followed him."** *(Mark 2:14; Enhanced)*

After the Draught of Fishes, Matthew or Levi's life was forever altered. On a given morning Simon and his fishing crew reported to the publican Levi that they had labored all night long and had caught nothing *(Luke 5:5)* . . . so there was really nothing for him to tax. And then, later on within that same day Jesus borrowed Simon's boat to minister to a large crowd on the shoreline of the Sea of Galilee. Subsequent to the ministration, and at the request of Jesus to let down the net, Simon and his partner Zebedee brought in two full boatloads of fish *(Luke 5:7)* to be weighed and accounted for. Levi is the one that they must report to for taxation.

The next day, or two at the most after that, Jesus calls Peter and Andrew as they are casting a net . . . and then further on down the shoreline the brothers James and John as they are repairing the net that had previously broken because of the prior catch of fish being so large. *(Matthew 4:18-22)*

And once that Jesus gathers the two sets of brothers, because Jesus had already asked Levi to follow him, Levi readily submits to Jesus' petition to join the entourage and now once again there are five disciples.

"**After these things came Jesus and his** *five new* **disciples into the land of Judea** *for a short period of* *time*; **and there he tarried with them** *and began to teach* *them about spiritual ministration*, **and baptized** *all those* *that would come unto him.*

And John *the Baptist* **also was baptizing** *people for* *the preparation of their heart* **in** *the springs outside the town of* **Aenon near to Salim, because there was much wa-ter there. And they** *all* **came, and were baptized.**

For John was not yet cast into prison.

Then there arose a question between some of John's disciples and the *local* **Jews about purifying.**

And they came unto John, and said unto him, Rabbi, he that was with thee beyond *the* **Jordan** *River*, **to whom thou** *personally* **bearest witness** *to him* *as being from God*; **behold, the same** *man* **baptizeth** *others*, **and all men come** *un*to **him** *instead of thee.*

John answered and said, A man can receive nothing, except it be given *unto* **him from heaven.**

Ye yourselves bear me witness, that I said, *that* **I am not the Christ, but** *rather* **that I am sent be-fore him.**

He that *actually* **hath the bride is the bride-groom. But the friend of the bridegroom, which** *is* *who I am* **standeth** *at the door of the chamber* **and heareth him** *upon the consummation. And he* **rejoiceth greatly**

because of the bridegroom's voice of the covenant confirmation. *This my joy therefore is fulfilled.*

He must increase from now on, *but I must decrease* from the scene.

He that cometh from above, is above all. He that is of the earth is earthly, and speaketh of the earth; he that cometh from heaven is above all.

And what he hath seen and heard, that he testifieth of; *and no man receiveth his testimony.*

He that hath received his testimony hath set to his seal that God is true.

For he whom God hath sent speaketh the very *words of God; for God giveth not the* Holy *Spirit by measure unto him.*

The Father loveth the Son of Man dearly, *and hath given* authority over *all things into his hand.*

He that believeth on the Son of Man, whom God hath sent, *hath everlasting life: and he that believeth not* on *the Son* of Man whom God hath sent *shall not* ever *see life; but the wrath of God* is destined to *abideth* up*on him* forever. *(John 3:22-36; Enhanced)*

As soon as Jesus has a core-group of disciples, early ministry training needs to commence. He takes the troupe and leaves the Galilee region and heads back down south into the Samaria region and the waters around the town of Aenon.

Originally, John was the only one who was baptizing repentant hearts in water as a preparatory action. That very vehicle of water baptism was used by God to reveal to His Prophet who the ordained Messiah for the Nation of Israel was.

But now that Jesus is on the scene, and actively involved in ministry with others, he is instructing his disciples in a hands-on manner concerning all of the different aspects of ministering to people. Water Baptism *(John 3:22)* . . . Exorcism *(Luke 8:27-33)* . . . Healing *(Matthew 8:14-16)* . . . Natural Need Necessities *(Luke 9:12-13, Matthew 17:27)* . . . Raising of the Dead *(Mark 5:35-42)* . . . Controlling of the Weather *(Matthew 24-27)* . . . and all of the other practical application situations that exist amongst the Society of Human Beings. The disciples are not simply groupies and stunned observers to the Miracle-Man of Nazareth as he goes about wandering all over the countryside of Israel performing supernatural exploits . . . they are students-in-training of the Master Professor.

Jesus said, *"**Verily, verily, I say unto you, He that believeth on me, the** practical **works that I do shall he do also; and greater works than these shall he do: because I go unto my Father.**"*
(John 14:12; Enhanced)

In a similar way, we are to step up to the plate in a Christ-Like manner with practical applications, to deal with the various situations that exist amongst the society of Human Beings today. We are the *Christ-on-Site* for today. *(II Corinthians 6:14-16)*

*"**And these signs shall follow them that believe** on me**; In my name shall they cast out** the tormenting **devils; they shall speak with new** unknown **tongues;***

*   **They shall take up serpents** that attempt to harm them**; and if they** unknowingly **drink any deadly thing, it shall not hurt them;** and **they shall** go forth amongst Mankind and **lay hands on the sick, and they shall recover.***" *(Mark 16:17-18; Enhanced)*

Are we casting out tormenting devils? Are we speaking with new unknown tongues? Concerning serpents and deadly drink, **"Thou shalt not tempt the Lord thy God"** *(Luke 4:12)* so snake handling and drinking strychnine are <u>not</u> activities that are prompted by God to prove faith. But God's protection is still valid and active should we find ourselves in a compromising position of danger. Are we laying hands on the sick amongst Mankind and thanking God for the healing? Are we controlling the weather at various times? Do we believe on God for His intervention if there is not enough to eat? And how many other notations can be made concerning what we as sons and daughters of the Most High God should be doing while we are still here on this Earth?

However . . . rather than continue to travel through the Scriptures and note every incident in the life of Jesus of Nazareth walking successfully as a Man, let us move on to explore how Jesus *The Christ* dealt with the specter of DEATH . . . both on the spiritual and on the physical level.

Dealing With the Specter of Death

I f we were able to stand at the threshold of ever-lasting past, and peer into the eternity of *future-time* that is set out before us, we would be able to see a tremendously brilliant light that out-shines all of the others, off in the distance. As we set our course and begin our journey, that light becomes our guide and the focal-point of our purpose.

If we were able to stand at a designated point that is eons away in the future from today and turn around and peer into the corridor of *expired-time*, we would be able to see a tremendously brilliant light off in the distance of days-gone-by, that out-shines all of the others. As we ponder all of that which has occurred to bring us to where we are at, that light becomes our reflection and the recognized focal-point of the resolve.

The resurrection of Jesus Christ of Nazareth from the Spiritual and Physical Dead can illustratively be compared to the detonation of a Super-Nova star explosion . . . and is in fact that tremendously brilliant light that out-shines all of the others that we have observed from a distance of both past and future. The resurrection of Jesus Christ is that very light and ***the*** focal-point of all of everlasting.

May we take just a moment, and step back into a position of observation from the point of the completion of the material portion of creation and the original first step of the moral creation? A chronological over-view of what God has accomplished would be . . .

- God has brought forth an entire universe of harmony . . . and there is a flowing stream of unity betwixt all things created. *(Psalms 19:1-6)*

- At a given point in time, a specific moral-angelic creature entertains iniquity and ultimately rebellion occurs. *(Isaiah 14:12-14, Ezekiel 28:15-16)*

- A *First Probational*-time is determined for the then current rebellious moral creations to reconsider their bad decisions. *(Romans 9:28)*

- When that *First Probational*-time concludes, all of the bad decisions become locked-down and additionally irreversible. *(Revelation 20:10)*

- The first Judgmental-action occurs at the conclusion of the *First Probational*-time and the corporate headquarters of the rebellion is destroyed. *(Genesis 1:2, Psalms 104:5-7, Jeremiah 4:23-26, and II Peter 3:5-7)*

- At that particular time there is no current locale of incarceration to put the rebels into . . . so their travel visas are suspended and their activities are severely limited.

- A specific locational-compound is then prepared to house all of the rebellious spirit beings because of God's stirred anger . . . but immediate incarceration into that compound is postponed because there is a *Second Probational*-time that lies directly ahead. *(Deuteronomy 32:22, Matthew 25:41)*

- A Superior-moral creation is brought forth *in* the image and *after* the likeness of the Creator Himself. *(Genesis 1:26, Psalms 8:3-6)*

- The suspension is lifted on the activities of the rebellious populous and they actually become an eternal contributing factor concerning free-will decision for Mankind. *(Romans 6:16)*

- The *Second Probational*-time begins and there is a departure from the established Righteous-Plan for Mankind almost immediately.
  (Genesis 2:17, Romans 5:12)

- At a point in time two-thousand years ago there was a drawing near to, and a close approach concerning, the tremendously brilliant light that lay directly ahead. *(Luke 1:30-33, Galatians 4:4)*

- Because of the extensive God-ordained authority of Mankind universal-alteration is now at the doorstep and the God/Man Jesus Christ of Nazareth becomes the center of attention. *(John 1:29-34, Hebrews 1:1-2)*

- At the moment of his *New-Spiritual-Birth* the Super-Nova explosion occurs and the tremendously brilliant light becomes manifest and etched into the corridors of reality. *(II Corinthians 5:16)* A new law is burned into the eternal law-books, *(Romans 8:2)* and new Spiritual-Life and immortality are now made available for Mankind. *(I Corinthians 15:53, II Timothy 1:10)* And upon his resurrection from the *Physical-Dead*, a New, unprecedented, super-natural, program is established. The *New Creation Body of Christ* project begins construction by the General Contracting First Person of the Godhead. *(I Corinthians 12:18)* The project-managing Second Person of the Godhead, as a Man, establishes a governmental structure and appoints department heads for the purpose of company unity and harmony. *(Ephesians 4:11-12)* And the power-demonstration Third Person of the Godhead takes up His pledging *"I will never leave you nor forsake you"* position as the manifestor of company policy and product manufacturing. *(Hebrews 13:5)*

Did Jesus Really Die Spiritually?

"*A nd about the ninth hour* of the day ***Jesus*** *cried* out *with a loud voice, saying, Eli, Eli, lama sabachthani? That is to say, My God, my God, why hast thou forsaken me?*" (Matthew 27:46; Enhanced)

The First Person of the Godhead and the Second Person of the Godhead have enjoyed complete, uninterrupted, and intimate spiritual harmony and fellowship from the unending corridors of Before the Beginning. At a point in time rebellion and disruption of universal harmony occurred because of the entrance of the Law of Sin . . . but the harmonious fellowship between the first two Members of the Godhead was uninterrupted and unaffected.

Additionally, rebellion and disruption from unrestricted Sin bled over into the creation of Mankind, because of the actions of the first Man named Adam . . . but the harmonious, intimate fellowship between the first two Members of the Godhead was still not altered or affected.

When the time finally came for the actual working out of the physical details, concerning the Plan of Redemption and the Second Person of the Godhead steps into an *Earth-Suit* of flesh to become Jesus Christ of Nazareth . . . that harmonious, intimate fellowship yet still remained intact.

However . . . when, **"he who knew no sin was made to be sin"** on the altar of the cross, *(II Corinthians 5:21)* and Spiritual-Death occurred through sacrifice and Law of Sin indebtedness, *(Romans 6:23)* the intimate sweet fellowship between the First Person of the Godhead and the Second Person of the Godhead, in the person of the Lord Jesus Christ, was broken . . . and Jesus cries out from the cross the manifestation of that breach.

Jesus' declaration is not simply a statement of frustration, or one of emotional upheaval. It is because of the fact that a solemn spiritual severance has taken place. Our focus must needs be taken off of just the physical if spiritual truth and reality is to be understood. Spiritual fellowship between two intimate kindred spirits has suffered devastating disruption and a cry of anguish echoes forth unto the heavens.

"All we like sheep have gone astray, we have *all* **turned every one to his own way; and the Lord hath laid** *up*on **him the iniquity of us all."** *(Isaiah 53:6; Enhanced)*

Chapter 53 within the Book of Isaiah is the chapter that makes notation on issues concerning the Messiah of Israel. The verse above within the chapter elucidates on the reality of what sin effects and causes within Human Beings. We are all Spiritually Dead in our sins, *(Romans 3:23)* and require the work of the cross to redeem us back unto life. Jesus bore the iniquity of all of Mankind, and when he did, it killed him . . . spiritually. *(Hebrews 2:9)* He paid the debt for the Law of Sin *invoice* that he did not owe, and we are the beneficiaries of that payment.

"I will declare the decree: the Lord hath said unto me, Thou art my Son; this day *of Rebirth* **have I begotten thee."** *(Psalms 2:7; Enhanced)*

This Psalms verse is a major notation concerning the Spiritual Death of Jesus of Nazareth. It operates hand-in-hand with the prophetical declaration that is given in II Samuel 7:14 . . .

"I will be *unto him* **his father, and he shall be** *to me* **my son."** *(II Samuel 7:14a; Enhanced)*

This statement is one of a future tense. **"I <u>will be</u> his father; and he <u>shall be</u> my son."** And even though the subject person within the chapter pages is King David, he is later noted as being a servant in verse five, and not a son. The prophetical reference within the statement is directed toward the Man Jesus

Christ of Nazareth concerning the days that lay yet ahead.

* * *

- The Second Person of the Godhead is God within His own right . . . <u>not</u> the Son of God. He is Immortal and His name is "The Word." *(John 1:1)*

- The Second Person of the Godhead, The Word, puts on a *Human-Suit* of flesh at a point in time and becomes a Man. He is no longer able to be Immortal when He does so, but has become Eternal of necessity, just like the first Adam. His name is Jesus of Nazareth. *(John 1:, Luke 1:30-31, and I Corinthians 15:45-46)*

- The God/Man, Jesus of Nazareth, is not the Son of God, he is indeed God, clothed in a *Human-Suit* of flesh. *(Hebrews 2:17)* His condition as a God/Man is not a result of a birth but rather of an incarnation. *(John 1:1; 14)*

- The God/Man, Jesus of Nazareth, is rejected by the very people that he came to redeem and is condemned to death by the leadership. *(John 1:11, 11:50)*

- The God/Man, Jesus of Nazareth, while he is hanging on the cross of Calvary is spiritually made to be Sin. *(Isaiah 53:6, II Corinthians 5:21)*

- The God/Man, Jesus of Nazareth, spiritually being made Sin, dies spiritually because of what Sin effects. *(Romans 6:23)* He is now no longer Eternal but has become Mortal because of his Spiritual Death. Moreover, being now Mortal he is able to physically die as well.

- When the legal and spiritual demand of the Law of Sin is met, the God/Man, Jesus of Nazareth, is *Begotten* and Spiritually Birthed into a New Creation condition within the region of the damned, and resurrected from the Physical Dead. *(II Samuel 7:14, Psalms 2:7, John 3:3; 5, Acts 13:33, Colossians 1:15; 18, Hebrews 1:5, and Revelation 1:5; 3:14)* A new spiritual law of *Life in Christ Jesus* becomes established as a higher law, to override the Law of Sin and the Spiritual Death that goes with it; and that law becomes active and operative for any and all that would choose to accept it through the reality of a Spiritual *New Birth*. *(John 3:3; 5, Romans 8:2)*

- The God/Man . . . New Creation . . . Jesus of Nazareth, upon his Spiritual *New Birth* becomes the **Only Begotten** Son of God . . . within his existence capacity of Humanity . . . as a Man. *(John 1:14; 18; 3:16; 18, Acts 13:33, Hebrews 5:5; 11:17, and I John 5:1)* He has effectively dealt with the devastating spiritual Law of Sin issue and has provided an escape from bondage, death, and separation from God. *(Romans 8:2)*

- The God/Man . . . New Creation . . . Jesus of Nazareth, upon his *New Birth* is no longer the same as he was before his death. *(II Corinthians 5:16)* He is __not__ a Jewish man any longer, but he has become a New Creation. *(II Corinthians 5:16, Galatians 3:28, and Colossians 3:11)* He is no longer a Mortal Man but has become Immortal once again. *(II Timothy 1:10)* He does not dwell within a Physical Body any longer but has been glorified and now inhabits an upgraded Spiritual Body. *(I Corinthians 15:44)*

"For thou wilt not leave my soul in the abode of *Hell; neither wilt thou suffer thine Holy One to see* physical *corruption."* *(Psalms 16:10; Enhanced)*

- Hell is a locale that was specifically prepared for the rebellious devil and his angels. *(Matthew 25:41)*
- All men during the *Probational Period for Mankind* are born Physically Alive but Spiritually Dead because of the Law of Sin. *(Romans 5:12; 6:23)*
- All men during the *Probational Period for Mankind* who do not take advantage of Spiritual Rebirth *(John 3:3; 5)* shall remain Spiritually Dead and shall ultimately be consigned to the prepared abode

known of as the Lake of Fire within the locale of Hell. *(Matthew 25:41, John 5:29)*

- Since the person that is referred to in Psalms 16 . . . who does not suffer physical corruption is indeed Jesus Christ of Nazareth, he is also the same person that shall not remain in Hell.

- The Spiritual Rebirth of Jesus established a new Law of *Life in Christ Jesus*, *(Romans 8:2, Colossians 1:18, and Revelation 3:14)* and *cuts-the-trail* for Spiritual Rebirth for any Human Being that would choose to follow his lead. *(John 3:3; 5)*

"The sorrows of death compassed me about, and the floods of ungodly men made me to be afraid.

The sorrows of Hell compassed me about: the snares of spiritual death prevented me from escape.

In my distress I called upon the Lord, and cried out unto my God: he heard my voice out of his temple, and my cry came before him, even into his ears." *(Psalms 18:4-6; Enhanced)*

It should be obvious that this excerpt from the Book of Psalms is prophetic and not real-time. The author is speaking about death, and the ramifications of death, and yet he is still very much Physically Alive upon the Earth at the time of the declaration. That it is prophetical indicates that the subject matter within the psalm does not apply to the man that wrote it, but rather unto another . . . specifically what the God/Man, Jesus Christ of Nazareth, would one day experience.

The subject is Death. The sorrows referred to are not physical sorrows because the body of the individual contains no life and is impervious to any kind of pain or sorrow. Spiritual Death is what holds the sorrows and pains within the confines of Hell. Jesus of Nazareth experienced the *sorrow*, the *fear*, and the *distress* that was connected to him tasting of death for every man. *(Hebrews 2:9)*

"He that is our God is the God of salvation; and unto God the Lord belong all of **the issues** resulting **from death."** *(Psalms 68:20; Enhanced)*

This is an example of a prophetical-declarative-statement. It is a statement of declaration, concerning an *issue* that God Himself is going to have to take the full responsibility for and secure a resolve. That *issue* is Death. Foreknowledge knew about it, so it is God that needs to fix it.

There are three conditions or states of *Death* that are in existence . . .

1) . . . The reality of Spiritual Death, which is a by-product and consequence of the Law of Sin. *(Romans 6:23)* Spiritual Death is an entry-level, incurable condition that accompanies Physical Life for all of Mankind. *(Romans 3:23; 5:12; 6:23)* The only provided *antidote* for Spiritual Death is the Spiritual Rebirth spoken of by Jesus of Nazareth to Nicodemus the religious Pharisee. *(John 3:3; 5)*

2) . . . The ultimate consequence of Spiritual Death is the incurable condition of the Physical Death of the Terrestrial Body that men occupy. When the allocated number of years expire, concerning a man's tenure on the planet Earth, the Terrestrial Body reaches a point where it ceases to function properly and Physical Death is the end result. The only provided *antidote* for Physical Death is a bodily Resurrection. For the *antidote* to become permanent the resurrection must be unto life. *(John 5:29)*

3) . . . The forever-condition of Eternal Spiritual Death is that which automatically occurs to any individual within the *Probationary Period for Mankind* that does not

accept the free gift of Spiritual Rebirth, and ultimately dies physically. Eternal Spiritual Death is a permanent, incurable, spiritual condition and there is no *antidote* that has been provided for it. *(Revelation 20:11-15)*

The *Second Death* *(Revelation 20:14)* referred to in the Book of Revelation is a second Physical Death occurrence that becomes a reality for those who are resurrected unto damnation. *(John 5:29)*

Please note that what is being talked about within the quoted Psalm are the issues **from** Death . . . the consequences that come with the Law of Sin and the conditions of Death that it brings. The only Being in the entire universe who could accomplish a resolution for so enormous and serious a problem was God Himself in the person of the Lord Jesus Christ. The responsibility to make all things right belongs to God. God turned the tables on Spiritual Death and brought *"life and immortality to light."* *(II Timothy 1:10)*

"The sorrows of death compassed me about, and the pains of Hell gat hold upon me: I found myself in trouble and in sorrow.

Then I called upon the name of the Lord; O Lord, I beseech thee, deliver my soul from this death." (Psalms 116:3-4; Enhanced)

Once again we have a prophetical declaration within the Book of Psalms. A real-time Spiritually Dead . . . Physically Alive man uttering words of fact under the inspiration of the Holy Spirit of God, hundreds of years before the actual fulfillment takes place.

"Set me as a seal upon thine heart, as a seal upon thine arm: for love is *as* strong as death; . . ." *(Song of Solomon 8:6a; Enhanced)*

The Song of Solomon gives us a testimony concerning the strength of death. In order for one to defeat an enemy *(I Corinthians 15:26)* one must be as strong as, or stronger than, the foe. Because of the strength of the Law of Sin and the conditions of Death that come with it, there is a requirement that only *Love* can bring an effective resolve. *(Corinthians 13:8)* We learn from the Scriptures that God is *Love.* *(I John 4:8)* Spiritual Death must be defeated, and to do that requires the tasting of Death itself, *(Hebrews 2:9)* by something or someone that is stronger than Death.

"He will swallow up *spiritual* death in victory; and the Lord God will wipe away *the* tears from off all *of the* faces; and the rebuke of his *own* people shall he take away from off *of* all *of* the earth: for the Lord hath spoken it." *(Isaiah 25:8; Enhanced)*

The Scriptures declare that God is *Light*, *(I John 1:5)* and that God is *Love*, *(I John 4:8)* and that God is *Life*. *(John 1:4; 5:26; 6:48; 14:6, Acts 3:15, and I John 1:2; 5:11)* Although it is grammatically incorrect there is a tremendous difference between **who you is** and **what you has**. God has omnipotence, and omniscience, and omnipresence, and is self-existent from everlasting . . . but that has absolutely nothing to do with His Personage.

On the cross of Calvary *Light* hung suspended . . . and was snuffed out by the darkness of Sin. On the cross of Calvary *Life* hung suspended and was swallowed up by the power of Spiritual Death. On the cross of Calvary *Love* hung suspended and was not able to be touched by either the darkness or the power of Spiritual Death. So when the full spiritual debt that Sin demanded was paid *Love* emerged triumphant . . . the *Light* was turned back on . . . and the *New Life* turned the tables around and swallowed up Spiritual Death in victory. *(Isaiah 25:8)*

"Therefore will I divide *unto* **him a portion with thc great, and he shall divide the spoil with** *all of* **the strong; because he hath poured out** *his* **soul unto the** *power of spiritual* **death: and he was numbered with the transgressors** *in his crucifixion;* **and he** *spiritually* **bare the sin of many, and made intercession for the transgressors** *against* **God."** *(Isaiah 53:12; Enhanced)*

The Scripture is **not** declaring that Jesus **"poured out his soul"** unto Physical Death. It is true that Physical Death was involved, but only after Spiritual Death had occurred. If you are not Spiritually Dead in origin, you cannot Physically Die. Established and ordained laws are involved. The physical does not override the spiritual . . . ever; even if we cannot understand it, and do not personally know how it works. He **"bare the sin of many"** by being **"made"** Sin. *(II Corinthians 5:21)*

"Him, being delivered by the *religious* **determinate counsel and** *prophetical* **foreknowledge of God, ye have taken, and by** *your* **wicked hands have crucified and slain:**

Whom God hath raised up *to life once again***, having loosed the pains of** *spiritual and physical* **death: because it was not possible that he should be holden of it."** *(Acts 2:23-24; Enhanced)*

Jesus of Nazareth is the person who was crucified and slain.

Upon Physical Death, before the resurrection of Jesus Christ of Nazareth, all men went to Hell . . . no exceptions. If you were considered righteous you went into a spiritual-comfort compartment within the locale, known of as *Paradise* or *Abraham's Bosom*. If you were unrighteous you went into the compartment locale known of as *Sheol* or *Hades* which is the arena of spiritual torment and pain.

Jesus being loosed from ***"the pains of death"*** indicates that he did not just go into the spiritual-comfort compartment to pay for the sins of all of Mankind.

The Spiritual Death of Man requires spiritual payment of the debt that the Law of Sin demands. You cannot purchase a spiritual product using physical coinage. The damage that was done by Adam occurred within the Realm of the Spirit, and so the repair of the damage must take place within the Realm of the Spirit as well.

"Know ye not, that so many of us as were baptized into *the mystical body of* ***Jesus Christ were baptized into his death*** *reality?"* *(Romans 6:3; Enhanced)*

As believers in Jesus Christ we did not pass from death unto life, *(1 John 3:14)* and receive the New Spiritual Life that we have by simply being baptized into the Physical Death of Jesus. Physical Death will avail nothing. New Spiritual Life is available for us because someone not under the curse that Spiritual Death causes, tasted of Spiritual Death for all men. *(Galatians 3:13, Hebrews 2:9)*

"For since by one man came the reality of death, by one man came also the resurrection of the dead.

For as in the Man named Adam all died, even so within Christ Jesus shall all be made alive who will receive it." (I Corinthians 15:21-22; Enhanced)

Within the annals of Scriptural record the Spirit of Truth relays to us concerning Mankind . . . that Spiritual Death came first and was followed by Physical Death. *(Genesis 2:17; 2:7b; 5:5)* And in addressing the issue of resolution for the problem, speaks of Physical Death first, and then of Spiritual Death, in the Scripture above.

The *antidote or cure* to any Physical Death issue is a Physical Resurrection for the body. *(John 5:29)* A Human man on this Earth is the one who started the Physical Death process . . . so a Human man must fix the problem and be the first one to be physically resurrected.

When we see that *"in Adam all die"* . . . it is referring to the Spiritual Death reality that originally occurred within the Man named Adam when he disobeyed God. The *antidote or cure* for all Spiritual Death is a Spiritual Rebirth. *(John 3:3; 5)* Adam was the first Man to Spiritually Die and Jesus of Nazareth is referred to as being the *"last Adam."* *(I Corinthians 15:45)* And, it is through Jesus that the opportunity for men to be made alive was given. However, *all* men shall not avail themselves of that offer.

*"And so it is written. The first Human man named **Adam was made a living soul** after he spiritually died; the last **Adam** named Jesus **was made a quickening spirit** when he was raised up from the dead.*

Howbeit that was not done first which is spiritual, but that which is natural and temporal; and afterward that was done which is spiritual and eternal." (I Corinthians 15:45-46; Enhanced)

A truth often missed by many is that Man was not originally created as a living soul, *(Genesis 2:7b)* but rather **became** a living soul when he Spiritually Died as is confirmed in the Scripture above.

The last Adam, which was the Man named Jesus of Nazareth, was Spiritually Alive from the corridors of everlasting . . . until he was *"made to be sin"* *(II Corinthians 5:21)* and *"tasted death for every man"* *(Hebrews 2:9)* and was spiritually separated from the heavenly Father. *(Mark 15:34)*

Foreknowledge knew of Man's rebellion so God legally proceeded with the flawed natural in order to lead us unto the flawless spiritual, through the work of the cross of the Lord Jesus Christ . . . in particular his Spiritual Rebirth and Physical Resurrection.

"For the love of Christ constraineth us; because we thus judge that if one man died for all other men, then were all the other men dead:

And that he died for all *other men***, that they which** *choose to* **live** *in him* **should not henceforth live unto themselves, but unto him which died for them, and rose again."** *(II Corinthians 5:14-15; Enhanced)*

If there was one who died for all and tasted death for every man *(Hebrews 2:9)* then the *all* that were dead were not Physically Dead but rather Spiritually Dead. And the Death that he tasted for every man was Spiritual Death and not simply Physical Death.

Now being Spiritually Alive because of a *New Birth (John 3:3; 5)* and Physically Alive on this planet, they now should not just live for themselves but for him who provided Spiritual Life and rose from Physical Death as well.

"To wit, that God was in *the* **Christ, reconciling the** *entire* **world unto himself, not imputing** *or holding* **their trespasses unto them; and hath committed unto us the word of reconciliation** *to take unto others***."** *(II Corinthians 5:19; Enhanced)*

God was in Christ. Christ was . . . and is still, God. *(John 1:14)* God became a Man without forfeiting being God. Jesus Christ is the God/Man that became the *Lamb of God* that was necessary for the ultimate sacrifice that was needed for the Law of Sin. *(John 1:29)*

The *reconciliation* that was necessary, and that God instituted, was because of spiritual separation. Spiritual separation occurred because of Spiritual Death. *(Romans 5:19)*

"For he hath made him to be sin for us *who were sinful,* **who knew no sin** *himself;* **that we might be made the** *actual* **righteousness of God in him."** *(II Corinthians 5:21; Enhanced)*

The someone who **"knew no sin,"** *(Romans 3:23)* which could *only* be the Lord Jesus Christ, was made to be sin *(II Corinthians 5:21, Romans 6:23)* . . . and in so doing tasted of Spiritual Death for every man. *(Hebrews 2:9)* Jesus went to the depth of where no other man could go to, and still survive, so that a way of escape could be established for whosoever would choose to accept it. *(John 3:16)*

"Who is the *very* **image of the invisible God, the firstborn of every** *New* **Creature:"** *(Colossians 1:15; Enhanced)*

Image and *Likeness* are given unto us within the first chapter of Genesis. In brief layman's terms, *Image* is talking about what is on the inside and *Likeness* is talking about what is on the outside.

This verse is revealing to us that a man has once again been able to become like God on the inside . . . just as Adam was originally created to be. *(Genesis 1:26)*

Jesus of Nazareth has dealt with the Law of Sin and has *cut the trail* for the whole world to follow him unto the redeemed **"conformed to his image"** condition. *(Romans 8:29)* This process is able to take place because of a Spiritual Birth. *(John 3:3; 5)* Adam disobeyed and became Spiritually Dead just like God had said that he would. *(Genesis 2:17)* Jesus of Nazareth as the sacrificial *Lamb of God* became legally Spiritually Dead *(Isaiah 53:6, Romans 6:23, II Corinthians 5:21, and Hebrews 2:9)* so that a legal Spiritual Birth and installation of a new law could take place. *(John 3:3; 5, Romans 8:2)*

It should not take rocket science for us to understand that **"firstborn of every creature"** is not referring to the natural or the physical realm. This is a statement of spiritual truth. The *translator-added* italicized word of *New* set before the word *Creature* would bring further clarity to the declaration.

"And without controversy *or debate* **great is the mystery of godliness:** *the Personage of* **God was manifest in the flesh** *through the person of Jesus Christ of Nazareth,* **justified** *and declared not guilty* **in the Spirit** *within the citadel of Hell,* **seen of angels** *upon his resurrection,* **preached unto the Gentiles** *because God is not a respecter of persons,* **believed on in the world** *through the testimony of men,* *and* **received up into glory** *until his promised return."* *(I Timothy 3:16; Enhanced)*

"God was manifest in the flesh." *(John 1:1; 14)* If that manifestation was not the unique Nazarene man named Jesus Christ . . . then who was it?

God in the flesh was *"justified in the spirit."* *(Romans 8:33)* In order for one to become justified . . . one must first become guilty. There is no justification that is needed for one who is already innocent. God became guilty in the person of the Lord Jesus Christ, of all of the things which other men have done. And upon full payment of the debt, Jesus the God/Man was justified within the spirit and was spiritually raised up unto *New Life,* *(John 3:3; 5)* and then he physically resurrected and rose from the dead.

God in the flesh was *"seen of angels."* *(Matthew 28:5-7, John 20:12-13, and Acts 1:10-11)* The risen Lord of glory was seen again and again by angels after his resurrection. Angels bore witness that indeed Jesus was risen from the pain and bondage that accompanies death in all of its conditions or states.

God in the flesh was *"preached unto the Gentiles."* When the church was first established, people of a Jewish persuasion were the only people at the beginning to hear the good news of what Jesus had done. But a number of years later the Gentiles began to hear about what God in Christ had done through the *"foolishness of preaching,"* *(Romans 1:16, I Corinthians 1:21)* the Roman soldier Cornelius being the first to be noted within the Scriptures. *(Acts 10:1-8; 24-45)*

God in the flesh was ***"believed on in the world."*** *(II Thessalonians 1:10)* The gospel has gone out into all of the Earth, *(Colossians 1:5-6)* and men and women everywhere have responded to the preaching of the Word of God.

God in the flesh has been ***"received up into glory."*** *(Acts 1:9; 3:20-21)* From corporate headquarters in heaven Jesus captains the ship that we now know of as *The Church*. Two-thousand years have come and gone and a prophetical promise is soon to be fulfilled in his returning for those who have received him as their personal savior and are still ***"alive and remain."*** *(I Thessalonians 4:17)*

"For unto which of the angels said he at any time, Thou art my Son, this day have I begotten thee? And again, I will be to him a Father, and he shall be to me a Son?" *(Psalms 2:7, II Samuel 7:14, and Hebrews 1:5)*

Both the Book of Psalms and the Book of II Samuel are quoted within this verse. II Samuel is a prophetical declaration of future spiritual realities, and Psalms 2 specifies a specific day that certain spiritual realities will take place. When we add Acts 13:33 to the mix, the picture gels and becomes quite clear.

"God hath fulfilled the same unto us their children, in that he hath raised up Jesus again; as it is also written in the second psalm, Thou art my Son, this day have I begotten thee." (Acts 13:33)

One does not **birth** from Physical Death into Physical Life . . . that process is called a Resurrection. (John 5:29) Nicodemus also thought that everything was on the physical level, and he was in error. (John 3:4) Jesus of Nazareth was not **begotten** unto Physical Life; however he was **begotten** unto Spiritual Life again, as a *New Creation* by God the Father utilizing the power of the Holy Spirit.

"Wherefore, as by one man named Adam sin entered into the world for a second time, and Spiritual Death came by sin. And so Spiritual Death passed upon all men, for that all men have sinned and come short of the glory of God:" (Romans 5:12; 3:23; Enhanced)

"For the wages of, and payment for, and consequence of sin is Spiritual Death. But the gift of God through the New-Birth is eternal life through Jesus Christ our Lord." (Romans 6:23; Enhanced)

"For since by a Human man came Spiritual and Physical Death into this world, by a Human man named

Jesus of Nazareth **came also the resurrection of the dead.** *" (I Corinthians 15:21; Enhanced)*

"But we see Jesus, who was made *in his Humanity . . . because of Adam's imposed servitude through his transgression,* *(Romans 6:16)* **a little lower than the angels for** *the purpose of* **the suffering of** *Spiritual* **Death.** *Being* **crowned with glory and honour** *upon his resurrection from that death.* **That he by the grace of God should taste** *of Spiritual* **Death for every** *single* **man** *amongst* **Mankind.** *" (Hebrews 2:9; Enhanced)*

"Forasmuch then as the *future* **children** *of the Most High God* **are partakers of flesh and blood, he also himself likewise took** *the flesh* **part of the same; that through** *the tasting of Spiritual* **Death he might destroy him that had the power of** *both Spiritual and Physical* **Death, that is, the devil.** *" (Hebrews 2:14; Enhanced)*

"I am he that liveth, and was dead; and behold, I am alive forevermore, Amen. And I have the keys of Hell and of Death. *" (Revelation 1:18; Enhanced)*

* * *

DEATH is the issue. DEATH is the problem. DEATH is the enemy. DEATH captures . . . and never releases. DEATH presents finality. DEATH must be dealt with . . . definitively!! And, who is going to handle that little problem? Who is going to deal with that evil specter?

It is truly amazing how blasé the Human creature has become about the reality of DEATH. How about you? Are you blasé about DEATH? Are you content to die? Is it an issue that really does not bother you that much? Do you honestly believe that when your *time* comes . . . because you think that you are a comparatively *nice* person . . . or because you profess that you *believe* in God . . . or because you belong to a particular religious *group* of individuals . . . that at your funeral you are going to be eulogized right up into heaven by the minister and your close friends? Are you fully resigned to the specter of DEATH as being an unavoidable part of *life?* Why??

God did not create Man to die. God created Man to live as long as He is going to live. DEATH does not come from God. DEATH comes from Sin. DEATH is an enemy of God. *(I Corinthians 15:26)* And, it is the last enemy that shall be destroyed.

* * *

"In the fulness of the time," *(Galatians 4:4a)* the Second Person of the Godhead agrees to divest Himself of several *non-transferables*, put on a *Human-Suit* of flesh encapsulating himself within the physical parameters-of-operation that are required concerning a Terrestrial body, patiently walk amidst a steady stream of rejection, finally surrendering himself unto hatred, and tasting of Spiritual and Physical Death . . . all for the sake of genuine Love.

In a *Kangaroo Court* manner, Jesus of Nazareth, after he is arrested within the Garden of Gethsemane, is shuffled around all night long. Beginning with religious Jewish ruler ship . . .

- ***Brought Before Annas:*** *(As a Jewish High Priest, Annas was appointed to that position at the age of 36. He was deposed by a man named Valerius Gratus nine years later, who was the procurator of Judea at the time. He was succeeded by his son-in-law Caiaphas who was a wealthy-class-resident of the upper portion of the city of Jerusalem. The ruling House of Annas had no less than eight members of this family holding the supreme High Priest office . . . Annas . . . five of his sons . . . his son-in-law Caiaphas . . . and his grandson Matthias who ruled from the year 65 AD. until the Diaspora.)*

   "Then the band *of men* **and the captain and officers of the Jews took Jesus, and bound him.**

DID JESUS REALLY DIE SPIRITUALLY?

And led him away to Annas first; for he was father-in-law to Caiaphas, which was the high priest that same year.

Now Caiaphas was he, which gave his counsel to the Jews of the religious hierarchy, that it was expedient that one man should die for the people rather than that the whole nation should perish." (John 10:50; 18:12-14; Enhanced)

"The high priest then asked Jesus of his disciples, and of his doctrine.

Jesus answered him, I spake openly to the world. I ever taught in the synagogue, and in the temple, whither the Jews always resort. And in secret have I said nothing.

Why askest thou me? Ask them which heard me, what I have said unto them: behold, they know what I said.

And when he had thus spoken, one of the officers which stood by struck Jesus with the palm of his hand, saying, Answerest thou the high priest so?

Jesus answered him, If I have spoken evil, bear witness of the evil: but if well, why smitest thou me?

Now Annas had sent him bound unto Caiaphas the high priest." (John 18:19-24)

- ***Brought Before Caiaphas and the Sanhedrin:***
  (Caiaphas Joseph was surnamed Caiaphas and was the Jewish High Priest from 18-37 AD. . . . The Sanhedrin was an aristocratic senate that was composed of both Jewish priesthood and laity representatives who were of pronounced Persian and Greek occupational histories stemming from the 4ᵗʰ century BC. They were the highest court of law to which the provincial courts of Judaism turned, for decisions in particularly difficult cases.

  Caiaphas may have been afraid of both the demonstrated power of Jesus of Nazareth and the attitude of the Galilean pilgrims who considered Jesus a hero . . . as we consider the swiftness of Jesus' trial before the Sanhedrin. To conduct a trial of capital charges at night was illegal. To continue the trial, and not acquit the defendant, when witnesses for the prosecution cannot agree, was illegal. For the person in charge to invite the criminal to convict themselves of their accused crime was illegal. The Messianic claim of Jesus was the focused assault and condemnation to death was the desire, which prompted Caiaphas to intervene and cross-examine the prisoner himself, when the original charges failed and the case was falling apart.)

  "And they that had laid hold on Jesus led him away *from Annas and took him* **to Caiaphas**

the high priest, where the scribes and the elders were assembled." (Matthew 26:57; Enhanced)

"Now the chief priests, and the *elders, and all* of *the council, sought* to bring *false witnesses against Jesus, to* be able to *put him to death;*

But they *found none* that could agree. *Yea, though many false witnesses* were petitioned and *came, yet found they none* that could agree. *At the last came two* other *false witnesses,*

And said, This fellow said, I am able to destroy the temple of God, and then *to re-build it in* only *three days.*

And the high priest arose from his chair, *and said unto him, Answerest thou noth-ing? What is it which these* witnesses do *wit-ness against thee?*

But Jesus held his peace. And the high priest answered and said unto him, I adjure thee by the living God that thou tell us whether thou be the Christ or not, *the Son of God.*

Jesus saith unto him, Thou hast truly *said. Nevertheless I say unto you* now, *Hereafter shall ye see the Son of man sitting*

on the right hand of power *on high***, and coming** *again* **in the clouds of heaven.**

Then the high priest rent his clothes, saying, He hath spoken blasphemy; what further need have we of witnesses? Behold, now ye have heard his blasphemy *yourselves.*

What think ye? They *all* **answered and said, He is guilty of death.**

Then did they spit in his face, and buffeted him; and others *of the servants* **smote him with the palms of their hands,**

Saying, Prophesy unto us, thou *that profess to be* **Christ. Who is he that smote thee?** *(Matthew 26:59-68; Enhanced)*

* **<u>Brought Before Pontius Pilate for the First Time:</u>** *(Pontius Pilate was a man who was about the same age as Jesus of Nazareth. He ruled from 26 to 36 AD., and was the fifth Roman procurator over the regions of Judea, Samaria, and Idumea. He was a proud, hot-tempered, obstinate and aristocratic young man, capable of childish behavior when his will was opposed, and as military-minded as his name suggests. His official place of residence was the seaport city of Caesarea on the Mediterranean coastline. His wife, Claudia Procula, was the granddaughter of the Roman Emperor Augustus Caesar.*

Ultimately, Pilate was outwitted and outmaneuvered by an older and craftier Caiaphas, concerning the Jesus of Nazareth Affair. He was a perfect stooge for Satan, and has been branded Scripturally and historically ever since as the condemner of Jesus.)

"Then led they Jesus from Caiaphas un-to the Roman **hall of judgment: and it was early; and they themselves went not into the judgment hall, lest they should be defiled; but that they might eat the Passover.**

Pilate then went out *of the judgment hall* **unto them, and said, What** *kind of an* **accusation bring ye against this man?**

They answered and said unto him, If he were not a malefactor, we would not have delivered him up unto thee *in the first place.*

Then said Pilate unto them, Take ye him, and judge him according to your law. The Jews therefore said unto him, It is not lawful for us to put any man to death.

That the saying of Jesus might be *thus* **fulfilled, which he spake, signifying what** *kind of a* **death** *that* **he should die.**

Then Pilate entered back **into the judg-ment hall again, and called Jesus** *unto himself,* and said unto him, Art thou the King of the Jews?

Jesus answered him, Sayest thou this thing of thyself, or did others tell it thee of me?

Pilate answered *unto him*, Am I a Jew? Thine own nation and the chief priests have delivered thee unto me: what hast thou done?

Jesus answered, My kingdom is not of this world. If my kingdom were of this world, then would my servants fight, that I should not be delivered to the Jews. But now is my kingdom not from hence.

Pilate therefore said unto him, art thou a king then? Jesus answered; Thou sayest that I am a king. To this end was I born, and for this cause came I into the world, that I should bear witness unto the truth. Every one that is of the truth heareth my voice.

Pilate saith unto him, What is truth? And when he had said this, he went *back* out again unto the Jews, and saith unto them, I find in him no fault at all." *(John 18:28-38; Enhanced)*

- **<u>Brought Before King Herod the Tetrarch:</u>** *(Herod Antipas is the second surviving son of Herod the*

Great, and ruler of the Galilee and Perea regions from 4 BC. until 39 AD., at which time he was summoned to Rome and banished. He is noted as being a vicious man who was idle and extravagant. He built the town of Tiberius on the north-west bank of the Sea of Galilee, which became his capital and residence.

Jesus was sent to Herod Antipas when Herod was in Jerusalem for the Passover celebration, but Jesus was under no obligation to verbally respond to him either legally or spiritually.)

"When Pilate heard *mention* **of** *the region of* **Galilee, he asked whether the man were a Galilean.**

And as soon as he knew that he belonged unto Herod's jurisdiction, he sent him *straightway* **to Herod, who himself also was at Jerusalem at the time.**

And when Herod saw Jesus, he was exceeding glad. For he was desirous to see him of a long season, because he had heard many things of him; and he hoped to have seen some miracle done by him.

Then he questioned with him in many words; but he answered him nothing.

And the chief priests and scribes *that were with Herod* **stood and vehemently accused him.**

And Herod with his men of war set him at naught, and mocked him, and arrayed him in a gorgeous robe, and then *sent him* back *again to Pilate.*

And the same day Pilate and Herod were made friends together; for before they were at enmity between themselves." (Luke 23:6-12; Enhanced)

- **_Brought Before Pontius Pilate for a Second Time:_** *(Pilate becomes aware that the case against Jesus is fraudulent. And he begins to recognize that he is expected to act as a destructive tool of the Sanhedrin. He suggests the customary Passover amnesty but has forgotten about the incarcerated Barabbas. Foiled in his escape-from-blame purpose by the Barabbas fiasco, and fearing the increasingly angry crowd, Pilate has to rethink the situation. Jesus is returned unto Pilate from Herod in mock regalia, and combined with Pilate's reluctance to condemn Jesus; he is led to have the Messiah scourged to placate the gathered people.*

  Upon being scourged by the soldiers, Jesus is taken to the guardroom or quarters before being returned unto Pilate. There the soldiers vent their detestation as an occupying force, by heaping upon this representative of a subjected race, who has called himself a king, their amassed frustrations. Illustrations of these actions still exist in the variety of knuckle-boards and hopscotch designs covering several flagstones at the foot of the stairs even unto today.

Pilate is convinced that Jesus is innocent. But as he goes out before the crowd again, even before he can speak, the Jews declare "If you release this man, you are not Caesar's friend; everyone who makes himself a king sets himself against Caesar." When Pilate hears these words Jesus' fate is sealed. He brings Jesus out and sits down on the judgment seat called Gabbatha, or The Pavement. He asks "Shall I crucify your King?" and the chief priests reply "We have no king but Caesar."

Outmaneuvered by a people whom he had not even begun to understand, and with his already precarious reputation in Rome dangerously threatened, and additionally being deafened by the clamorous blood-lust of the crowd, Pilate resigns, signs the death warrant and hands Jesus over for crucifixion.)

"Now at that Passover **feast the governor was wont to release unto the people a prisoner, whom**soever **they would.**

And they had then within the jail **a notable prisoner, called Barabbas.**

Therefore when they were all **gathered together, Pilate said unto them, Whom will**

ye that I *should* release unto you? Barabbas or Jesus which is called *the* Christ?

For he knew that for envy they had delivered him.

When he was *therefore* set down on the judgment seat, his wife *Claudia* sent unto him, saying Have thou nothing to do with that just man: for I have suffered many things this day in a dream because of him.

But *when* the chief priests and elders *heard these things, they* persuaded the multitude that they should ask *for* Barabbas, and *demand that* Pilate destroy Jesus.

The governor answered and said unto them, Whether of the twain will ye *choose* that I *should* release unto you? They said *unto him,* Barabbas!

Pilate saith unto them, What shall I do then with *this* Jesus which is called *the* Christ? They all say unto him *with one accord,* Let him be crucified.

And the governor said, Why, what evil hath he done? But they cried out *even* the more, saying Let him be crucified.

When Pilate saw that he could prevail nothing, but that rather a tumult was *being* made, he took water, and washed his hands *before the multitude, saying I am innocent of the blood of this just person: see ye to it.*

Then answered all of the people, and said, His blood be upon us, and upon our children.

Then released he Barabbas unto them: and when he had scourged Jesus, he delivered him up to be crucified." (Matthew 27:15-26; Enhanced)

We have now reached the threshold. The Creator-God of the universe is about to be slain because of the blatant errors of MAN. The Sinless is about to be made Sin. The finest creature of all of the creation that has ever come forth, has run completely amok, and in order to salvage divine design, divine expectation, divine hope, and divine desire . . . God Himself, must now step up to the plate, and personally taste of the heinousness of death. *(Hebrews 2:9)*

Most of the time the average Christian man or woman does not even realize what is at stake when Jesus of Nazareth is about to be crucified. Physical, physical, physical is all that we hear about. Physical, physical, physical is all that we are shown. Physical, physical, physical is all that is put forth for us to think about. The priceless reality-adjustment that lies just ahead is <u>not</u> about the physical . . . it is about the spiritual. If the spiritual realities are dealt with correctly, then the physical consequences will be able to take care of themselves . . . automatically. The spiritual is what existed first . . . and then the physical came later. The spiritual is that which has the ascendency and is the primary . . . the physical is secondary. God has always been a spirit . . . and Man started out as a spirit, but became physically-soulish right at the get-go, *(Genesis 2:7)* because of his spiritual demise. *(Genesis 2:17)* God, who is spirit . . . put on the physical . . . to definitively deal with the actual spiritual realities . . . so that the physical operations would be corrected . . . automatically. That poignant time has now finally come.

"To wit, that *the Personage of* **God was in** *the* **Christ,** *for the purpose of* **reconciling the world unto himself, not imputing** *or holding* **their trespasses unto them. And** *he* **hath** *since,* **committed unto us the word of reconciliation** *to take unto others." (II Corinthians 5:19; Enhanced)*

On a rugged cross, atop the hill called Calvary, on the outskirts of the city of Jerusalem, the God/Man named Jesus of Nazareth was literally made Sin. All of the vileness within the depths of darkness . . . and all of the lies and subterfuge which continually persist . . . and all of the sexual perversion and wickedness that men wallow in . . . and the totality of the heinousness of all of that which is foul, is suddenly attached like shards of metal to an electrically charged magnet . . . and Jesus cries out in anguish . . . *"Eloi, Eloi lama sabachthani?"*

Holy is made to be unholy. Pure is made to be foul. Sweet is turned to bitterness. Expectation becomes despair, and Jesus is plunged into the depths of the hopelessness that pools at the farthest reaches of the void of bottomlessness. The spiritual reality that most people are completely unaware of, is that Jesus went into the Region of the Damned in my place . . . and that he went there FOREVER! It was not a three-day and three-night *cakewalk* as most people suppose . . . it was a FOREVER reality.

The ordinary Christian will not ever be able to understand that particular spiritual truth without a direct revelation from the gracious Spirit of Truth Himself. Jesus traded places with you and me on a FOREVER level. Only the prophetical life of Jonah the prophet, and the prophetical declarative statements of *"three days and three nights"* (Jonah 1:17, Matthew 12:40; 27:63, Mark 8:31; 14:58, and John 2:19-20) grants the Father God in heaven the legal right to raise Jesus of Nazareth up from the dead exactly seventy-one hours, fifty-nine minutes, and fifty-nine seconds from the time of his entombment.

The Super-Nova Resurrection

Special Notation: *Definition of a Super-Nova: "One of the rarely observed nova outbursts in which the maximum intrinsic luminosity of the explosion may reach one billion times the intensity of the sun." — Webster's Ninth New Collegiate Dictionary*

What Happened in the Spirit . . .

"Who is the *express* **image of the invisible God, the firstborn of every** *New* **Creature."** *(Colossians 1:15; Enhanced)*

"And he is the head of the body, the church: who is the beginning *of the New Creation,* **the firstborn from the** *spiritual* **dead; that in all things he might have the preeminence."** *(Colossians 1:18; Enhanced)*

"These things saith the Amen, the faithful and true witness, the beginning of the *New* **Creation of God."** *(Revelation 3:14; Enhanced)*

"And when I saw him, I fell at his feet as *if I were* **dead. And he laid his right hand upon me,**

saying unto me, Fear not. I am the first and the last.

I am he that liveth, and was dead; and, behold, I am alive forevermore. Amen. And now, I have the keys of Hell and of Death." (*Revelation 1:17-18; Enhanced*)

A Super-Nova explosion is the closest visual, physical-illustration that can be given concerning what spiritually took place within the bowels of this Earth, when the Holy Spirit of the Living God showed up in Hell, and imparted new *Life* into the Sin-saturated spirit of the deceased God/Man Jesus Christ of Nazareth.

Nothing short of the creation of a brand-new, supernatural, ultimately Supreme Human Being is what occurred spiritually within the Citadel of the Damned, and physically within the sepulcher of Joseph of Arimathea.

This MAN is now the culmination of the original divine design . . . errant correction and restoration necessity . . . and supreme authoritative exaltation of the apex of all creation. This MAN is a god. *(Psalms 82:6)* In particular, he is now the God/original god-MAN, once again. *(Please do not allow unknowledgeable-carnal thinking to rob you of this moment of revelation insight.)*

Sin cannot touch this MAN, and has absolutely no power over him at all.

Death cannot touch this MAN, and has absolutely no power over him at all.

Mortality cannot touch this MAN, and has absolutely no power over him at all.

Corruption cannot touch this MAN, and has absolutely no power over him at all.

This MAN is *Born-Again* (John 3:3; 5, I Peter 1:23) . . . this MAN is *Incorruptible* (I Corinthians 15:53) . . . this MAN is *Recreated* (Ephesians 2:10) . . . this MAN is *Resurrected* (Philippians 3:11) . . . this MAN is *Supernatural* (Matthew 17:20) . . . this MAN is *Immortal* (I Corinthians 15:53) . . . this MAN is *More Than a Conqueror* (Romans 8:37) . . . this MAN is *Blood-Related* to God (Ephesians 2:19) . . . this MAN is *Seated at the Right Hand* of Majesty on High (Ephesians 1:20) . . . this MAN is *The Express Image of God,* in the flesh (Hebrews 1:3) . . . this MAN is *Administrative* (Revelation 22:5) . . . this MAN is a *Household Member of the Family of the Most High God* (Ephesians 2:19).

And at the very point of his being brought forth as a New Creation Human Being, this MAN is unlike any other natural man that has ever been in existence in days gone by, and unlike any other natural man that will be coming forth into existence in the days that lie ahead. He stands alone. He is a beacon of newness, purity and love.

In addition, his return to *Life* has affected an alteration in actual *Time* calculation. Excepting for the Nation of Israel, who under the influence and direction of Satan, rejected and murdered this natural man in the first place, the entire world currently marks *time* from his exemplary work of redeeming Human-Beings from eternal death and destruction. There have been 2,015 years that have expired after his death. *(Anno Domini – A.D.)*

What Happened in the Physical . . .

"But Mary stood without at the *entrance of the* **sepulcher weeping. And as she wept, she stooped down** *and stepped* **into the sepulcher.**

And *as she did, she again* **seeth two angels** *dressed* **in white sitting, the one at the head, and the other at the feet, where the body of Jesus had lain.**

And they say unto her, Woman, why weepest thou? She saith unto them, Because they have taken away my Lord, and I know not where they have laid him.

And when she had thus said, she turned herself back *to leave the sepulcher*, **and saw Jesus standing** *in front of her*, **and knew not that it was Jesus.**

Jesus saith unto her, Woman, why weepest thou? Whom seekest thou? She, supposing him to be the gardener *because of the early morning hour*, **saith unto him, Sir,** *if* perchance **thou have borne him**

hence, tell me where thou hast laid him, and I will *come and* **take him away** . . . *turning and gesturing as she spoke to where the body had once lain.*

Jesus saith unto her, Mary. She, *suddenly recognizing his voice, excitedly* **turned herself** *back to face and embrace him*, **and saith unto him, Rabboni! Which is to say, Master!**

Jesus saith unto her, Touch me not! For I am not yet ascended *un***to my Father** *in heaven.* **But go** *un***to my brethren, and say unto them** *that* **I ascend unto my Father, and** *to* **your Father; and to my God, and** *to* **your God.**

Then, **Mary Magdalene came and told the disciples that she had seen the Lord, and that he had spoken these things unto her."** *(John 20:11-18; Enhanced)*

The *Born-Again* spirit/soul portion of the New Creation Jesus of Nazareth has now been reunited with his upgraded, glorified, Spiritual Body. The only wounds that remain are those which are Scripturally permanent forevermore . . . the piercing in the hands . . . the feet . . . and the lance thrust into his side. All of the other contusions and lacerations from the scourge and from the crown of thorns have been completely healed by the residue of the priceless remission-blood that remained within the natural Terrestrial body after his death. Rigor mortis to his flesh . . . and the normal blackening death-null of the physical blood . . . and general bodily decay was not even possible because of that incorruptible blood, and the eternal Scriptural declaration.

"For thou wilt not leave my soul in hell; neither wilt thou suffer thine Holy One to see corruption." (Psalms 16:10)

* * *

Additionally, the combining of the two verse notations below, testify to the extraordinarily new physical prowess that an upgraded, glorified, Spiritual Body is capable of:

"Jesus saith unto her, Touch me not! For I am not yet ascended unto my Father in heaven. But go unto my brethren, and say unto them that I ascend unto my Father, and to your Father; and to my God, and to your God." (John 20:1; Enhanced)
and . . .
"And they departed quickly from the sepulcher with fear and great joy. And they did run to bring his disciples word of his resurrection.

And as they went on their way to tell his disciples, behold, Jesus returned from depositing his blood on the Mercy

Seat in heaven, and he **met them, saying, All hail. And they came** *rejoicing* **and held him by the feet, and worshipped him,** *and he did not protest." (Matthew 28:8-9; Enhanced)*

"The power of his resurrection" *(Philippians 3:10)* has afforded dynamic supernatural changes within the now glorified, up-graded, Spiritual Body *(I Corinthians 15:44)* of the Lord Jesus. Within a short *time* window of less than twenty minutes, Jesus must <u>ascend</u> unto the dwelling place of God, which is the Third Heaven . . . deposit onto the Mercy Seat *(Hebrews 9:5)* within the Temple of God in heaven *(Revelation 3:12)* the residue of his priceless remission-blood that remained within his resurrected body . . . and return to meet and greet the *other women* who are still on their way to tell the disciples the good news.

These verses reveal to us that a resurrected, up-graded, glorified, Spiritual Body is able to fly under its own volition without any external aids . . . travel at an incalculable hyper-speed . . . and does not need any special equipment to penetrate and operate within outer-space.

* * *

Also worthy of notation is the fact that a resurrected, upgraded, glorified, Spiritual Body is not prohibited in its operational activities by solid walls, and additionally has the capacity to become invisible.

"Then the same day at the evening hour, being Sunday evening, the first day of the week, when the doors were shut and locked where the disciples were assembled for fear of the Jews, suddenly came Jesus and stood in the midst of the disciples, and saith unto them, Peace be unto you.

And when he had so said, he showed unto them his hands and his side as proof that it was really he, and that he was alive once again and risen from the dead. Then were the disciples glad, when they saw the Lord.

Then said Jesus unto them again, Peace be unto you: as my Father in heaven hath sent me to minister reconciliation, even so send I you to reconcile a lost and dying world.

And when he had said this, he breathed on them, and saith unto them, Receive ye the Holy Ghost; and they were all Born-Again within their spirit on that very day.

Whosoever sins ye remit, they are remitted unto them. And whosoever sins ye retain, they are retained." (John 20:19-23; Enhanced)

Of course, these notations apply directly to the risen New Creation Jesus of Nazareth. However, he is the official prototype of the upgraded model of the incredible new Human-Being creation that God has brought forth in raising up His Christ from the dead. He is the one who has cut the trail for you and me to follow. And we now belong to a race of God-class created creatures that will hold the supreme positions of authority, acting directly upon the commissions given from the Master Creator Himself.

Know We Him No More

"*W*herefore henceforth, *that is, from now on,* know we no man after the flesh: yea, though we have known Christ after the flesh, yet now henceforth, *that is, from now on,* know we him no more *the same way that we have known him before.*"
(*II Corinthians 5:16; Enhanced*)

Incredibly sad, is the spiritual reality that 21st Century Christendom does not seem to realize that this Revelation statement, made by the Apostle Paul to the believers within the city of Corinth, actually exists. And even sadder still, is the manifested fact concerning the world-wide genuine lack of recognition of the true identification of the *New Creation*, Lord Jesus Christ of Nazareth by his own followers.

What we continue to do, as a whole, is to observe the *Old Jesus* **"after the flesh"** within the Gospel accounts . . . but today, he is a *New Creation* . . . and so, **"know we him no more."** *(II Corinthians 5:16)*

What we continue to preach about, as a whole, is the *Old Jesus* **"after the flesh"** within the Gospel accounts . . . but today, he is a *New Creation* . . . and so, **"know we him no more."** *(II Corinthians 5:16)*

What we continue to study about, as a whole, is the *Old Jesus* **"after the flesh"** within the Gospel accounts . . . but today, he is a *New Creation* . . . and so, **"know we him no more."** *(II Corinthians 5:16)*

Practically speaking, on the whole, we do not even **"do"** a small portion of what the *Old Jesus* **"after the flesh"** told us to do *(John 14:12)* . . . and yet now, he is a *New Creation* . . . and so, **"know we him no more."** *(II Corinthians 5:16)*

So . . . what might be wrong with this picture concerning our modern 21st Century Christianity? Thank the Lord in heaven for his grace.

* * *

The Second Person of the Godhead, who is 100% God, because of a universal breach that was brought about by the Law of Sin . . . and by way of an incarnation, left Heaven and came to this Earth. *(John 1:14, Hebrews 2:14; 17)*

The Second Person of the Godhead, who is 100% God, after He had become incarnated, became an *original-Image (Hebrews 1:3)* within an *altered-Likeness (Genesis 5:3, Philippians 2:7)* and additionally became a 100% MAN. *(John 1:1-2; 14, Hebrews 2:17)*

The Second Person of the Godhead, who is 100% God, today, as an incarnated-MAN, is a 100% direct descendant from the first MAN named Adam. *(I Corinthians 15:45)*

The Second Person of the Godhead, who is 100% God, through the tasting of the condition of Spiritual Death, *(Hebrews 2:9)* repaired the immense universal breach that was brought about by the Law of Sin, doing so as a 100% MAN.

The Second Person of the Godhead, who is 100% God, upon repairing the immense universal breach as a 100% MAN, became a brand *New* type of Human-Being, upon his being raised-up from the Spiritual and Physical Dead that is 100% *different*. *(II Corinthians 5:16-18)*

This *different, New Creation* MAN is now **Born-Again** and is not the same type of Human Being as he was before his *New Birth*. *(II Samuel 7:14, Psalms 2:7, Acts 13:33, John 3:3; 5, and I Peter 1:23)* This *different, New Creation* MAN is a new **Recreated** species of the Human Being and is not the same as before his *New Birth*. *(Ephesians 2:10)* This *different, New Creation* MAN is **Immortal** and does not belong to the State of Eternal or Mortal anymore. *(I Corinthians 15:53, II Timothy 1:10)* This *different, New Creation* MAN is **Supernatural** and no longer restricted by the bounds of the natural realm anymore. *(Matthew 17:20)* This *different, New Creation* MAN is **Incorruptible** and shall never be subjected to decay or corruption of any kind, ever again. *(I Corinthians 15:53)* This *different, New Creation* MAN is **Seated at the Right Hand of God**, within the same throne as the Master Creator, which we know of as the Father. *(Ephesians 1:20)* This *different, New Creation* MAN is **Related** to the Godhead **by a Blood-bond**. *(Ephesians 2:19)* This *different, New Creation* MAN is **More Than a Conqueror** over the entire kingdom of darkness, and everyone that is in it. *(Romans 8:37)* This *different, New Creation* MAN is an ultimate **Express Image** of the Personage of God and has made it possible for redeemed men to become the gods that they are called within the Scriptures, and are expected to be. *(Psalms 82:6, John 10:34-36, and Hebrews 1:3)* This *different, New Creation* MAN is **Administrative** and shall exercise authority over every quadrant of the universe. *(Revelation 22:5)* This *different, New Creation* MAN is a **Household Member of the Family of the Most High God**, and shall dwell with God Himself forevermore. *(Ephesians 2:19)*

And because this *different* MAN is a *New Creation*, and not just the *Old Jesus **"after the flesh"*** that we are used to . . . the practical, continual, work-a-day reality within our modern 21st Century Christianity is that . . . ***"know we him no more."*** *(II Corinthians 5:16)*

* * *

Thank the Lord that there is still a possibility that we might be able to *catch-up* with what the Word of God has to say, and *close-the-gap* concerning our antiquated approach to spiritual reality issues. But it will not be as simple as ripe apples falling off of a tree and onto our heads. We must purpose to labor to enter into the rest that a gracious God has already provided. *(Hebrews 4:11)*

Step #1 — It is absolutely necessary that we renew our minds as the Word of God commands us to. *(Romans 12:2, Ephesians 4:23, and Colossians 3:10)* This is a real renewing of our minds that we are talking about here, and not simply the mental-accenting gobbley-goop that is put forth today in Christian circles.

We need to really *know* what the Word of God has to say on the everyday, nitty-gritty issues of life that men and women confront continually. We need to stop our religious denial and graduate from our infancy concerning *knowing how* to use . . . and then *actually* using the Word of God as the weapon of warfare that it was designed to be. *(II Corinthians 10:4, Hebrews 4:12)*

We need to have a genuine clarity concerning what ***"rightly dividing the word of truth"*** really means. *(II Timothy 2:15)* What God has written to the Nation of Israel and for the Nation of Israel is not necessarily written to you personally. On the heavenly *time*-table of fulfillment, the dealings that God has with the Nation of Israel *(within the RIGHT NOW)* are on the *Old* side . . .

and *(within the New Creation time-*table of fulfillment *of the RIGHT NOW)* you are on the *New* side.

Step #2 — We must come to a sobering place of reality and recognition that the *Old Man* and the *New Man* are __not__, and should not be, the same man. *(Ephesians 4:22-24)* Thinking the same way that I have always thought is no longer correct if I claim that I am *Born-Again*. Talking the same way that I have always talked is no longer correct if I claim that I am *Born-Again*. Acting the same way that I have always acted is no longer correct if I claim that I am *Born-Again*. What is it concerning the words *PUT OFF*, from the Book of Ephesians, that we do not understand? Foul language needs to stop! Lying needs to stop! Negative and defeatist thinking needs to stop! Bad behavior needs to stop! Incorrect attitudes, prejudices, jealousies, envy, and all of the heinous social manifestations from Hell, that currently permeate Christianity, and seem to pass as being *normal*, and that somehow we think are *ok*, need to STOP!!

Step #3 — Sin has always been ***the*** problem . . . and now that the *New Creation Jesus* has definitively handled the Sin problem by establishing a new, higher spiritual law named *Life in Christ Jesus (Romans 8:2)* . . . we need to **"lay aside every weight, and the sin which**

doth so easily beset us" *(Hebrews 12:1)* and run the race with patience, and keep our eyes on him.

Too many times we focus on what is happening all around us at the time. We continually pray the problem and not the solution, because we are unaware of what the Word of God has to say concerning what the solution really is. We are not supposed to be moved by the circumstances . . . we are to alter the circumstances by being the men and women of faith that God has called us to be. We are to walk by faith. *(II Corinthians 5:7)* We are to live by faith. *(Habakkuk 2:4, Romans 1:17, Galatians 3:11, and Hebrews 10:38)* As *New Creations* we have become people of faith by what *New Creation Jesus* has done for us.

The devil is not the one in charge, and we should not put up with his shenanigans any longer . . . we are the ones in charge because of the victory that we enjoy, living within *New Creation Christ Jesus*. And contrary to popular belief and declaration, God is not the One in charge either . . . we are the ones in charge because of who we now are within *New Creation Christ Jesus*. *(Isaiah 45:11, I Corinthians 15:24-28, Galatians 2:20, and Philippians 4:13)*

   Special Notation: *How long are we going to deny the clear testimony of Scripture, in lieu of some false humility statement, from some Christian icon, which is Scripturally ignorant concerning New Creation Realities?—How long?*

This is a *New* day of resurrection spiritual-empowerment. *(Philippians 3:10)* We have been enjoying this *New* day for the past two-thousand years, but have generally not taken full advantage of the spiritual-empowerment that has been granted. As a whole, we need to grow-up. We need to become responsible. We need to become accountable. We need to become persons of integrity, and honesty, and truth. And we need to do this soon. Time is running out quickly. We are in a Laodicean Age and it is rapidly coming to a close. *(Revelation 3:14-17)*

May we purpose to redouble our efforts and re-commit ourselves unto our loving heavenly Father. Accept tutorage, put away the pride, stop with the *"I know what the Bible says"* façade, purpose to learn, and rise up to be the **"manifestation of the sons of God"** *(Romans 8:19)* that we are suppose to already be. May the blessing of the Lord be upon you as you do.

The Family Business

"*That all men should honour the Son, even as they honour the Father. He that honoureth not the Son honoureth not the Father which hath sent him.*" *(John 5:23)*

"*For as the Father hath life in himself; so hath he given to the Son to have life in himself;*
And hath given him authority to execute judgment also, because he is the Son of man."
(John 5:26-27)

The *time* has come to put away the ever-pressing present, and the affairs which consume our thinking of the natural things that are here-and-now on planet Earth.

The *time* has come for us to consider the future, and the part that each and every one of us who are now *New Creatures in Christ* will play in the days ahead.

The *time* has come for us to put on the three-dimensional glasses of vision and begin to mentally and spiritually prepare for the responsibilities that we shall be privileged to shoulder.

New Creation Realities of the Pauline Revelation testify that the whole of Creation is actually a *Family Affair,* that we are universally involved with. We are today, the actual *Adopted Children* of the Most High God. *(Romans 8:15, Galatians 4:6)* We will forever dwell within our *Fathers Home*, the City of the New Jerusalem. *(John 8:35; 14:2, Ephesians 2:19)* Our individual bedrooms of repose are in actuality *Personal Mansions* that have been custom built to fit our heart's desire. *(John 14:2)* Shortly, we shall begin to co-reign over all of the affairs of life with the *New Creation Jesus* who is our big brother. *(Romans 5:17; 15:12, I Corinthians 15:25, II Timothy 2:12, and Revelation 5:10; 20:6; 22:5)*

Unless we are specifically assigned unto a governance position on this Earth, we will not continue to live on the Planet Earth anymore after the *Probation for Mankind* comes to a conclusion.

We shall be residentially abiding within the confines of the City of New Jerusalem, which is to be the *Universal Capital for Administration, Governance, and Maintenance*, and which shall be forever suspended somewhere above the atmosphere of this planet named Earth.

We shall be dwelling within our own personal mansions, with places to go and people to see and things to do within the city, and shall be on an *"on call"* basis for any universal administrative or maintenance issue that may need to be addressed. Our loving

Father will call upon a given child, to accomplish a specific task.

Glorified, upgraded, supernatural Spiritual Bodies shall be able to transport saints to any particular locale within creation parameters.

Because we will be *"conformed to his image"* (Romans 8:29) by that time, the Father can trust that the task completion shall occur without mishap, even as if His Only Begotten Son, Jesus *(Revelation 3:12; This author does not know his new name at this point in time)* were actually the person assigned to accomplish it.

We will be interfacing with, and dealing with, *Holy Angels* of various ranks concerning physical element adjustments, potential construction, needed tutorage, necessary scribing, and other issues of everyday life.

We will be observing and assisting *Other Creatures* as we visit and report on other habitable planets that are teeming with life throughout the wide expanse of this universe. Reports on progress and faithfulness shall be submitted to corporate headquarters for accurate record keeping.

The running of this universe will be similar to a large corporate conglomerate with various departments and authoritive levels, overseen by faithful employees, executing company policies meticulously.

Spiritual instruction concerning the Word of God shall continue ad infinitum for both saints and subjects of the Kingdoms. Personal training and advanced tutorage will occur on a regular basis for maximum growth and development.

It will be expected that each and every child of God will be dealt with respectfully by the *Holy Angels* and *Other Creatures* and natural *Human Beings*, just as Jesus stated in the Scripture quoted above. And any reports to the contrary will be considered an affront to the Master Creator Himself. *(John 5:23)*

Once again it is an appropriate *time* to share a vision that the Lord has given unto this author several years ago:

The time has come to begin the expansion. Probation was necessarily both painful and extremely sad, but now it is concluded and we can move on. 'Supernatural' sons and daughters of a loving heavenly Father have enjoyed over 1,000 years of personal training in the exercising of their faith, and in their on-the-job ruler ship maneuvers during the 'conforming' process, in becoming carbon copies of the Only Begotten. They have shared in judgment responsibilities and are now qualified to advance in their training. It is time for their honed skills to be demonstrated 'in the field.'

A call goes forth for a chosen child to report to the executive office for assignment. A Divine memo gives explicit and detailed instruction concerning planetary preparation of the intended new colony. Travel arrangements are diligently made and departure takes place toward the selected location.

Gliding through the star clusters and perspective worlds of the future is intoxicating beyond description. Colors exceeding brilliant, indescribable formations, and a virtual weaving in of gas and light, that pulsates hypnotically, is seemingly everywhere.

Arriving at the intended destination, a quick survey provides substantiation of what needs to be done. From a given locale on the surface of the planet, the son of glory utters decrees of adjustment to the elements of the atmosphere. There is no hesitation as to the compliance of the directive. Various gases begin to increase and then decrease, and ultimately reach a desired balance. Schematic wind circuitry, clouds for moisture administration, and the 'day' time and 'night' time necessities are brought unto a point of harmony.

The existing land formations are much too harsh to utilize, and certain portions of the mountains need to be relocated to provide for optimum benefit. Commands are given and the elements respond. Water is scarce, so established Basic Creation Elements need to be brought onto the scene and utilized to establish all that is needed for a pristine habitation.

A final global survey at the tasks end confirms that the new locale is now acceptable, and the ship of populous can arrive at their scheduled discretion. Colonization should be able to commence without any further difficulty.

A leisurely trip of return is quite relaxing, and upon reaching home the eternal mansion is indeed a welcomed sight. Aah, worship is scheduled for the morning, and hearts and hands shall be raised in exaltation of the Regent of Glory. Peace beyond understanding, love, harmony, joy, and fulfillment in every aspect of life once again permeates every fiber of his being. With assignment completed, his heart and his home have been united once again.

* * *

"And I will pray the Father, and he shall give you another Comforter, that he may abide with you for ever." *(John 14:16)*

For the most part, at this point in real time, we do not fully understand the depth of the statement that Jesus has made above.

Today, if we are *Born-Again*, we usually ignore the Holy Spirit that is living within us. We allow verbal rubbish to cascade out of our mouths unchecked. We set our eyes on seduction, nudity, and acts of privacy that are reserved for one man and one woman who are in a marital covenant relationship. Our ears are pummeled and drink in foul language from movies, TV, and societal neighbors, with little or no monitoring taking place.

We do not realize nor comprehend the power-generator that literally dwells within. We are more than conquerors *(Romans 8:37)* who are content to suffer defeat when the powers of darkness rear their ugly head. We are strengthened with all power and might on the inner man, *(Ephesians 3:16)* but prefer to focus upon the outer man and the demands that continually scream to be satisfied.

Jesus is currently working to present himself with a glorious church, *(Ephesians 5:27)* but we need to step away from all of the sinful trash and do our part if we want to see a fulfillment of that declaration.

Yielding unto the Holy Spirit classes need to commence and a concerted effort of purposing needs to occur soon. Let us not disappoint the One who gave his all for us . . . it is the least that we can do.

* * *

"For if by one man's offense death reigned by one; much more they which receive abundance of grace and of the gift of righteousness shall reign in life by one, Jesus Christ" *(Romans 5:17)*

"If we suffer, we shall also reign with him: if we deny him, he also will deny us." *(II Timothy 2:12)*

"And hast made us unto our God kings and priests: and we shall reign on the earth." *(Revelation 5:10)*

"Blessed and holy is he that hath part in the first resurrection: on such the second death hath no power, but they shall be priests of God and of Christ, and shall reign with him a thousand years." (Revelation 20:6)

"And there shall be no night there; and they need no candle, neither light of the sun; for the Lord God giveth them light: and they shall reign forever and ever." (Revelation 22:5)

The declarations are made. The mandate is clear. The fulfillment is near. Let us rise up to the position and the commission that our God has created us for. Appointed rulers of the universe arise, and take your place!

Maranatha!

Meet the Author

By-The-Book Ministries, Inc. began in 2001 as a teaching outreach. Rob E. Daley has been gifted by God to be able to explain biblical truths in an easy to understand manner.

Many have been blessed by his teaching style.

Rob was saved and filled with the Holy Spirit in 1978 and has been instructed by the greatest teacher of all—the Spirit of Truth Himself. Rob is an ordained minister with the Assemblies of God International Fellowship and has pastored in various churches over the past 34 years.

It is the desire of this ministry to see the body of Christ solidly taught, and grow up into the things of the Lord. Rob is available for seminars, retreats, conventions, etc.

Rob can be reached at:

thedaleys@bythebookministries.org

http://robdaleyauthor.com

www.ingramcontent.com/pod-product-compliance
Lightning Source LLC
Chambersburg PA
CBHW032137040426
42449CB00005B/281